Parent-teacher Associations

Edmondson, Edna Elder (Hatfield), Mrs. [from old catalog]

Foreword

THE very rapid development of parent-teacher associations in the last few years, their unique position among social organizations in the community, and their unusual opportunities for usefulness make it important that there be a proper understanding of their function their field of activities and their relations to other social organizations.

In the preparation of this pamphlet various sources of information have been drawn upon Publications of the National Congress of Mothers and Parent-Teacher Associations, of the Indiana Parent-Teacher Association, and of the Extension Divisions of Iowa and Wisconsin have furnished valuable suggestions Other sources of information have been reports and personal letters of local parent-teacher associations in Indiana and personal conferences with the state president of the Indiana Parent-Teacher Association.

Contents

PARENT-TEACHER ASSOCIATIONS—   PAGE

Purpose   5
Activities   8
How to Organize   12
County and City Parent-Teacher Councils   15
Joining the State and National Associations   15
Types of Schools   16
High School Parent-Teacher Associations   17
Rural Parent-Teacher Associations   17
Successful Parent-Teacher Associations   19

HISTORY OF THE MOVEMENT AND THE NATIONAL ORANIZATION—

History of Parent-Teacher Associations   22
History of the National Organization   22
  Organization   23
National Convention   23
Membership in the National Congress of Mothers   24
Founders' Day   24
Financial Support   24
The Child Welfare Magazine   24
Cooperative Arrangements with National Organizations   25

THE INDIANA PARENT-TEACHER ASSOCIATION—

History   26
  Organization   26
  Counties and Cities   27
Annual Convention   28
Membership and Affiliated Associations   28
State Organizer   28
Financial Support   29
Monthly Bulletin   29
Activities of the Association   29
Coöperative Arrangement with the Extension Division of Indi-
  ana University   30
Home Reading Courses in the Extension Division of Indiana
  University   30
Cooperation with the Indiana Child Welfare Association   31
Cooperation with the Indiana State Teacher Association   31

PAPERS READ AT THE STATE CONVENTION OF THE INDIANA PARENT-
    TEACHER ASSOCIATION—   PAGE
    President's Address   Mrs Hence Orme   32
    An Adventure in Rural Health Service   Miss Amalia Bengston   37
    Fundamental Concerns of the Parent-Teacher Association   L N
        Hines   41
    Physical Education in the Public Schools   George E Schlafer   43
    Safety First   H E Meginnes   46
    The State—An Offender   Judge James A Collins   47
    Mothers of Men   Mrs Alice French   52
    The Real Meeting-Place of Home and School   Rev Frank S C
        Wicks   54
    Vocational Guidance   G I Christie.   56
    Why Children Reach the Juvenile Court. Judge Frank J Lahr   63
    The Rural Schools   W. W. Black   68

APPENDIX—

    Survey of High School Life and Conditions in Fort Wayne, Ind.   70
    Suggested Constitution and By-laws for Local Parent-Teacher
        Associations (adapted from Constitution suggested by the
        Indiana Parent-Teacher Association and the Constitution and
        By-laws of the Rose Hill High School Parent-Teacher Associa-
        tion of Jeffersonville, Ind)   71
    Suggested Constitution for Parent-Teacher Councils in Counties
        and Cities (adapted from Constitution suggested by the
        Indiana Parent-Teacher Association and by the National Con-
        gress of Mothers and Parent-Teacher Associations)   73
    Constitution and By-laws of the Indiana Parent-Teacher Associa-
        tion   74
    Child Welfare Study Topics   .   79

Parent-Teacher Associations

PURPOSE

The purpose of the parent-teacher association is to bring the home and school together in the interest of the child

The home and the school are the two most important agencies in the training of children. With the differentiation of the school as a specialized institution charged directly with the education of children has gone a gradual growing apart of these two forces. As long as teachers "boarded round" a very personal relationship existed between the homes in the community and the school. Even after this custom ceased there were the gatherings of the parents at the school for pie socials spelling matches Friday afternoon exercises to hear the children "speak their pieces", and basket dinners on the "last day of school" to maintain this friendly personal relationship

But with the passing of these customs and the growing complexity of community life has come about a formal relationship between the home and the school characterized if not by actual hostility and a working at cross purposes, at least with a lack of understanding and indifference And yet the problems dealt with by the home and the school are the very ones for which a common standard of both institutions is necessary in the best interests of the child

Both institutions contribute to the training of the child and both should therefore cooperate in that training. The managers of these two institutions are the teachers and boards of education on the one side and the fathers and mothers on the other. The teacher has charge of the child about six hours out of the twenty-four, and the parents supposedly have charge of him the other eighteen hours—under the teachers about thirty hours a week for about thirty-six weeks of the year at best, and under the parents the rest of the time. An agreement of these two sets of managers on common policies and common methods would help greatly in bringing about the best results

If parents thoroly understand the school —by personal acquaintance with the teachers, by visiting the school during class work, by a study of the course of study—if they thoroly understand what the school work is, what the school is doing and trying to do for the child and the community, they can do many things to make that work effective. They are likely to be more sympathetic and appreciative of the efforts of the child. They begin to see their responsibility in helping along the work of the schools

In the beginning of his school life parents can help very much to adjust the child to his change of environment by picturing the school to him as a happy, desirable place to be rather than a place of severity and punishments. His change from the informal life of his home to the necessarily formal atmosphere of the schoolroom will be made much easier and the consequent task of the teachers much lighter if habits of obedience and respect for authority have been well grounded long before school age

Upholding the authority of the teachers in the presence of the child not only helps the teachers directly, by increasing respect for their own authority, but indirectly in their efforts to train the child to have a proper respect for all authority While the admonition of the pioneer father (not the mother be it noted) to his son, "If you get a lickin at school, I'll give you another at home", smacks more of severity than of reasonableness it can at least be partially justified on the ground of the principle involved and the intent back of it Refraining from criticizing the teachers in the presence of the child and never on the basis of the child's statements alone goes far toward retaining the respect of the child for his teachers An expression of interest and appreciation of the teachers' efforts shown by inviting the teachers into the home, or to a drive or to an entertainment helps to inspire the child with that same appreciation and with an increased loyalty to the teachers because of the evident friendship of his parents

Parents who are in full sympathy with the work of the schools will so arrange it that home conditions are conducive to the best school work Because no child can do effective school work unless he is in good physical condition, parents will see to it that children get plenty of sleep—children under fourteen at least ten hours—,that meals at home and home duties are so arranged that children do not have to hurry unnecessarily to get off to school, they will observe school regulations as to infectious diseases and school rules to protect the health of children, and will heed the advice of the school authorities as to any physical defects of children discovered at school Such parents will encourage punctuality and require regular school attendance, will show an interest in the child's school work, will require that home work be done if assigned and provide a quiet place for study free from interruptions and with good light, will confer privately with the teacher if the child is backward, and will dress the child simply, neatly and modestly.

These and many other specific ways in which they may be helpful will present themselves to parents who understand the schools and who are in sympathy with their efforts

On the other hand, the teachers who know the home environment, the home influence, and the parents point of view can teach the child much more effectively because of their enlarged opportunity for sympathetic and complete insight into his individual needs, capacities and potential powers They can do more in the six hours in which the child is under their care because they know the influences surrounding him the other eighteen They are able to make due allowance for the influence of the home in the case of good or poor school work and thereby know just where help is most needed They can treat with the child more wisely if they understand just which of his characteristics are probably due to his inheritance and which to his environment

By a complete understanding of home conditions, teachers are able to supplement home training in many important details They may emphasize those traits of character which have received least attention at home and need not stop to dwell at length upon those where home training is sufficient and successful They may foster cleanliness and neatness and modest, simple dressing; they may encourage consideration for others and urge an avoidance of slang or careless language. They can instil a regard for civic cleanliness, civic beauty, civic righteousness, a respect for property rights, and build up standards of right living in the place of poor ones or none at all. They can build up a knowledge of how to play by teaching games and fostering a love for them. They can discover if poor work in school is due to a lack of time at home to prepare lessons, or to other home conditions that might be adjusted. They can guard children's health by seeing that the schoolroom has proper ventilation, heat, and light; they can prevent children sitting on the ground in wet weather, sitting in school with wet shoes, and can notify parents of physical defects discovered at school.

These and many other specific ways of increasing their helpfulness in the training of children will occur to teachers who know the home conditions of the children in the schools.

SCHOOL FEEDING AT HUNTINGTON, IND.

The parent-teacher association is a modern social device for bringing parents and teachers together in frank, informal, friendly conference for a mutual understanding of the problems of the home and the school as related to children. It acts as a clearing-house of information between parents and teachers. Regular meetings on fixed dates save time and effort for both. The full free discussion possible there aids in establishing the mutually helpful relation that ought to exist between parents and teachers. Individual matters can be taken up as general problems, so as to give offense to none. Difficulties and misunderstandings disappear when discussed over a cup of tea. Meeting in this way, parents and teachers teach each other, and both have their points of view changed. Parents lose somewhat their highly over-personal attitude to their own children by an increased interest in all the children of the school, and teachers lose somewhat their highly impersonal attitude because of an increased interest in the children as members of individual homes.

ACTIVITIES

The parent-teacher association, as an association of parents and teachers organized in connection with the school, has for its field of activity the study and promotion of child welfare. Only subjects pertaining to that field can properly be considered by a parent-teacher association as such. Other subjects may be of deep interest to its members and may even be acted upon by them in their parent-teacher meetings as by any other organized group in the community, but such interest and such action are beside the purpose of the organization as a parent-teacher association.

For purposes of consideration by parent-teacher associations, problems in the general field of child welfare fall properly into three divisions: those of children of school age in the school and home, those of children under school age in the home, and those of children of any age in the community. The parent-teacher association, because of its peculiar function, its type of organization and its unique position in the community, is best fitted to deal with the problems of the first division—those of children of school age in the home and school—and reaches its highest degree of usefulness in the community when it clearly recognizes that fact and confines its chief activities to that set of problems. However, because of the close relationship of the problems of all three of these divisions—the child in the home and school, the child under school age, and the child in the community—because the same homes are touched by all these problems and because the school life of the child is so directly affected by all of them, it is not wise to draw the lines of differentiation too closely.

The ideal situation is that in which the parent-teacher association assumes a different relationship to each of these sets of problems: when it confines its activity in dealing with problems of children under school age to a study of those problems with the object of self-improvement, of fitting themselves as individual parents to deal more effectively with the problems of their individual children; when it confines its activity in dealing with the problems of children of all ages in the community to a study of those problems with the purpose of forming a background of intelligent public opinion and of cooperating in movements started by others in the community for the improvement of community conditions affecting children; when it reserves its chief activity for studying problems and directly initiating and carrying out undertakings for the improvement of conditions for children of school age in the school and the home. In the first case the association studies for the purpose of action as individuals, in the second case for cooperative community action as an organization, and in the third case for initiating action directly as a parent-teacher association.

Any study club or community organization can quite as successfully undertake the first two types of activity. But that which differentiates the parent-teacher association, which sets it apart and justifies its existence as a special type of organization, is its peculiar fitness to initiate and carry out undertakings to promote the welfare of children of school age in the home and school—undertakings designed to solve the problems which home and school parents and teachers working together alone can solve.

For study of child welfare problems in the two divisions where the parent-teacher association does not expect to initiate special undertakings as an association—problems of children under school age, and problems of children of all ages in the community—one of two methods may be followed either a special section for child study may be formed meeting at different times from the whole association, and reporting their work from time to time thru their chairman or each year one or two of the general meetings of the whole association may be given up to such study The former plan is better adapted to carrying on organized consecutive courses in child study For study and initiating definite undertakings for children of school age in the home and school, the whole association may be organized by committees working and reporting at each general meeting

Just what lines of study to follow and what definite undertakings to initiate and carry on must be governed by the special interests of the individual parent-teacher association and by local needs Parent-teacher associations differ in their personality and ways of working and neighborhoods differ as to their most pressing problems Careful study is always wise before determining what special undertakings to initiate and carry on Sometimes a survey of conditions is necessary before the general sense that "something ought to be done can be crystallized into a definite notion of just what ought to be done and how to go about it In the selection of work to be undertaken certain considerations must be taken into account it must be a vital and important work it must be well understood, definite, clear-cut plans must be laid for carrying it out once started it must be carried to a successful end

It is possible here only to suggest subjects for study and undertakings by parent-teacher associations for the welfare of children of school age in the home and school In the Appendix are given lists of references for study of the various topics listed here, as well as for study of problems of children under school age in the home, and of children of all ages in the community The following list of subjects includes also some suggestions for methods of work which have been found to be of practical value in parent-teacher associations

I A study of the state laws governing schools

The whole association may be divided into a number of small committees to report on various sections of the laws relating to the school system of the state This study is especially valuable in the beginning of the life of the organization to lay the foundation of a thoro understanding of the school system and a broad sympathy with its working

II A study of local school needs and methods of supplying them

A small committee may be appointed at the beginning of the year to secure from school superintendents, principals and teachers a list of the most urgent needs of the school The report of this committee may form the basis of further study of certain specific needs discovered and plans to satisfy those needs

III A study of the local school building

The preceding inquiry may have brought out certain needs in regard to the school building itself which require further investigation and committees may be appointed to make such. Various questions as to the building will naturally rise Is it large enough? Is a new building needed?

Are additions to the old one necessary? Is the building sanitary? Is its equipment sufficient for general teaching purposes in respect to blackboard space, seating space, maps, charts, and the like? Is its equipment sufficient and proper for certain special purposes as for domestic science, manual training, lunchrooms, restrooms, first aid facilities, and toilet facilities?

IV. A study of the local school grounds.

Committees may be appointed to make a special investigation and report on the school grounds. Such special questions will present themselves as the following: Are they large enough? Are they equipped for playgrounds? Are they planted with trees, shrubs, and bulbs to make them attractive?

V. A study of supervised play and recreation and physical education in the schools.

Committees may be appointed to make a special investigation and report on play, recreation, and physical education in the schools: Are there play supervisors and instructors in physical education? Are there

PLAY IN SCHOOL YARD AT BLOOMINGTON, IND.

playgrounds in the school yard? If so, are these equipped? What is the situation as to gymnastics and athletics? Are there play festivals, pageants, and folk dancing? Of special interest to parent-teacher associations in high schools is an investigation of high school social affairs and efforts to make them successful. Such problems as the following are ones on which teachers and parents of the pupils in the high school need to agree: the kind of social affairs to be given for high school pupils, the kind of social affairs to which they are allowed to go, the evenings on which such affairs are to be held, a general policy of chaperonage, simple dress for high school girls, reform of extravagant habits, simplified high school commencements. Agreement on a definite, uniform policy in such matters by all the teachers and all the parents will do much to keep the social life of the young people up to a high standard. It is alike demoralizing to the social standards of young people for a certain few parents to allow their children to attend social functions which are disapproved of by the great majority of parents in the community, as well as for a certain few parents to deny to their children privileges which the great majority of the parents approve and allow to their children

VI   *A study of health of school children and sanitation of the school building and grounds*

Committees may be appointed to study and report on such subjects as the following: health habits of school children—care of teeth, diet, sleep, clothing, exercise, general living conditions—,school feeding, school physician, school nurses, physical and mental examination of school children, sanitary conditions of the school building and yard—drainage, water supply, heating, ventilation, lighting, toilets, and general care of the building

VII   *A study of the school as a social center*

Committees may be appointed to study the subject, the school as a social center, and to report with recommendations to the association for action   This subject, while profitable to any parent-teacher association for study, is of especial importance to rural parent-teacher associations because of the lack of social life in many rural communities and because of the great need for the development of cooperative effort.   The school lends itself to the social center idea especially because of the possibility of enlisting there all classes of the children and adults in the community in civic welfare schemes   All sorts of social activities may be developed such as the following   athletic contests debating clubs discussion leagues declamation contests old-fashioned singing schools and spelling schools canning clubs poultry clubs potato clubs and garden shows   Such a school may become a center to bring out neighborhood resources of books, magazines, newspapers, and pictures that all may enjoy what each has   Visual instruction devices may be used in such centers for both information and entertainment   Entertainment features of meetings may be emphasized to a greater degree in rural associations than is justified in town and city associations

VIII   *A study of social hygiene*

Conferences on the wisest ways of dealing with questions of social hygiene may be held with small groups of parents   Opportunities for study of the subject may be the most helpful features of such conferences

IX   *A study of school attendance*

A committee may be appointed to make a study and report on the attendance of children at the local school   Other committees may study and report on the state attendance and state and federal child labor laws   and others the general subject of school attendance and the value of education   The investigation of attendance at the local school will include such questions as the following   Are children out of school who should be there?   What is the cause of such absence?   Is there a truant officer?   Is his work effective?   How many children are out on work permits?   Is there a continuation school for these children and are they attending?

How many children are repeating their grades? Is this because of absence from school or lack of ability or both?

X   *The school library*

A committee may be appointed to investigate and report the question of a school library. Is one needed or is there an adequate public library in the community? Has the public library plenty of reference books? Does it have magazines? Does it have books on child study and child welfare to lend to mothers? If there is no public library available, can a school library be started?

XI   *A study of thrift habits of school children*

A committee may be appointed to work out with the school officials plans to teach and encourage thrift in the schools. Teachers and parents may agree on some plan such as school savings bank or cooperation in the thrift plan of the U S Treasury.

XII   *A study of the present salary scale of teachers.*

A committee may be appointed to study the salaries of teachers both locally and in the country at large. This problem is an acute one thruout the country and there is need as never before for accurate information as to the facts and for calm consideration as to remedies.

XIII   *A study of the curriculum organization and administration of the school system*

Full appreciation sympathy and cooperation with the workings of the school can be had only by a full understanding of the curriculum, organization, and administration of the schools. Committees may be appointed to study and report fully and sympathetically to meetings on various phases of the school work.

One or two persons may report on the school fund—how great a proportion of the total tax it is, how it is divided, how it is administered. Someone may report on the school board—how it is constituted, whether there is a woman on the board. Committees may be appointed to study and report on such subjects as the following: the high school, the junior high school, the elementary school, kindergartens, vacation and continuation schools, open air schools and open air classes, ungraded rooms for backward children, vocational guidance in the school, health supervision, school nurses, dental clinics, school gardens. A committee may be appointed to examine and report on the course of study for the public schools of the state.

HOW TO ORGANIZE

Parent-teacher associations are organized according to the principles set out in Robert's *Rules of Order* (p 284 Robert's *Rules of Order*, Revised Edition, 1915) governing the organization of any permanent society, adapted to the special type of organization of the parent-teacher association. For the convenience of those wishing to organize such associations the details of organization are here given step by step.

Any group of fathers, mothers, or teachers may issue a call for a meeting to organize. As a preliminary step the interest, cooperation, and consent of teachers, principals, and school superintendents must be secured. Those most deeply interested should consult together and carefully lay plans   They should have had copies of sample constitution and by-laws of other associations for use in drafting their own. In consultation with the teachers and school officials they should select a date, preferably an evening date so the fathers can attend, which will not conflict with other business, social, or religious meetings in the community. The school should be chosen as the place of meeting if possible after having secured the consent of the school officials.

The meeting should be well announced. Invitations giving the purpose of the meeting should be sent by the children in the school to their parents. The following is a convenient form for this invitation: "Parents and friends of the ———— school are cordially invited to attend a meeting at (place) on (day, date, and hour) for the purpose of forming a permanent organization of parents and teachers of the school."

For this first meeting there should be a short, interesting program of music and community singing. Short exercises by the school children oftentimes mean a good attendance of parents. The exercises should be short and the children should be dismissed immediately after their part in the program, as the business of the rest of the meeting will be uninter-

CHILDREN ON A TEETER

esting to them, and their presence often prevents full and frank discussion of certain important matters to come before such an organization as a parent-teacher association.

When it is time for the meeting to open someone previously agreed upon rises and says, "The meeting will please come to order. I move that ———— act as chairman of this meeting." (The superintendent or principal of the schools is a good person to have act as chairman for this first meeting.) Someone in the meeting says, "I second the motion." The one who made the motion then says, "It has been moved and seconded that ———— act as chairman of this meeting. Those in favor of the motion say aye." The newly elected temporary chairman then takes the chair and says, "The first business in order is the election of a secretary. Nominations are in order." The temporary secretary is then elected as the chairman was and takes a seat near the chairman to keep a record of the proceedings.

The first business is the reading by the secretary of the call for the meeting. The chairman then calls on someone to state the object of the meeting. Someone interested in forming the association should then introduce the speaker who may be an outside speaker secured for the purpose, or some local speaker. This speaker should give briefly the history of the parent-teacher association movement, the purpose and the purpose and activity of parent-teacher associations, and should present convincingly a number of well thought out reasons for forming such an association. The speaker may even outline at this time some definite course of study or suggest some special undertaking much needed for the welfare of the children, as a special reason for organizing at this particular time. Brief descriptions of what other similar associations have done often stimulate interest. The speaker should urge the importance of joining the state and national organizations at the beginning. Following this should be an informal discussion of the matter. Several persons should be ready to speak (by previous arrangement) and the chairman may call on other members of the meeting to give their opinion.

When a sufficient time has been spent in this way someone should offer a resolution such as the following: "Resolved, that it is the sense of this meeting that a parent-teacher association shall be formed for (*state purpose broadly*)." Upon the adoption of this resolution a committee of usually three or five should be appointed by the chairman to draft a constitution and by-laws and to report at the next meeting. (For suggested constitutions for local parent-teacher associations see Appendix.)

A motion is then made to adjourn to meet at a certain time and place, or to take a recess of twenty or thirty minutes to allow the committee time to prepare the constitution and by-laws. This latter method is usually preferable because it allows all the business of organization to be completed at one time. If the preliminary work has been done carefully the committee for the preparation of the constitution and by-laws will already have at hand sample constitutions and by-laws so that their decision can be quickly made.

When this committee is ready to report the meeting is again called to order as previously by the chairman the officers of the first meeting serving until permanent officers are elected. The chairman calls for the reading of the minutes of the previous meeting, and asks for corrections or suggestions. If there are no corrections the chair announces that the minutes stand approved as read. If there are corrections the chairman instructs the secretary to make them and then announces that the minutes stand approved as corrected.

The first business is the report of the committee on the constitution and by-laws. The chairman of this committee reads the constitution and by-laws, and moves their adoption. When this motion is seconded and the chair has stated the motion he then orders the secretary to read the constitution section by section, asking after each section is read "Are there any amendments to this section?" If there are any amendments they are voted on at once and included in the section. When the entire constitution has thus been read and amended section by section, the whole constitution as amended is read. The chairman then throws the entire constitution open for amendment when other sections may be inserted if desired. The vote on the adoption of the entire constitution as amended is taken, a majority vote being necessary to adopt. The by-laws are then adopted in the same manner.

The next business is the election of permanent officers of the association according to the provisions of their by-laws. It is a good plan to choose for president a parent, for vice president the principal of the school, for secretary a parent, and for treasurer a teacher, thereby distributing the responsibilities among parents, teachers, and school officials. As each officer is elected he takes the place of the temporary one With the adoption of the constitution and by-laws and the election of permanent officers, the organization is complete.

Arrangements should be made at this meeting for a committee to have charge of the programs and conduct the business of the association The principal of the school may ask the teacher of each room to select a mother or father to represent that room and these parents, together with the officers and the teachers of the various rooms, may form a very satisfactory committee The general work of the association may be done by committees so selected as to employ the abilities and to develop the latent capacities of the greatest number of members These committees should be appointed with regard to the chief interests of the members, each committee carrying on some important phase of the work

COUNTY AND CITY PARENT-TEACHER COUNCILS

Where there are three or more parent-teacher associations in any given county or city, parent-teacher councils may be formed in the county or city in order to coordinate the efforts of the individual associations The state parent-teacher association will organize and recognize such councils Each council adopts its own constitution and by-laws and elects its own officers (For suggested constitution for county and city parent-teacher councils see Appendix) Only one council may be formed in any one county (outside of cities) and only one in any one city. The council should hold no more than three meetings a year There should be no dues in the council, but voluntary offerings may be made

Members in any one association belonging to the council are automatically members of the council No important action should be taken by the council without approval by the state parent-teacher association

JOINING THE STATE AND NATIONAL ASSOCIATIONS

Membership in the state association automatically carries with it membership in the national association The best time to join the state and national association is at the time of organization Application for membership should be made to the state association, which sends blank membership forms On receipt of these the local treasurer sends the names and addresses of the officers and members of the local association in duplicate to the treasurer of the state association together with dues The state treasurer sends a receipt for dues to the local treasurer enters the names and amounts on the books and forwards one list of names to the state headquarters where the association is listed with the others affiliated with the state and national association and where the lists of members are kept on file as the state membership The state treasurer forwards a duplicate list of the names and addresses of officers and members of the local association together with half the dues to the national treasurer, retaining half the dues in the state treasury for the expenses of the state association The national treasurer then sends to the state treasurer the required number of membership cards for each member of the local association, which cards are forwarded by the state treasurer to the local treasurer

There are a number of reasons for membership in the state and national association From the point of view of the local association perhaps the most important reason is that of its permanence and success Experience has shown that in most cases scattered, isolated associations neither live very long nor accomplish much in their work Affiliation with the state and national association lends life to local associations because it affords a possibility for the exchange of ideas Practical suggestions based on the experience of others are sent out by the state and national associations In many states a leaflet or bulletin is issued at regular intervals to enable local associations to keep in touch with present-day movements and methods (In Indiana a mimeographed bulletin is sent out from state headquarters the first of each month containing matters of interest to the associations of the state) Local associations feel an added strength and courage by the knowledge that they are a part of an organization composed of many units like themselves with the same purpose, working on the same kinds of problems toward the same end, meeting with similar discouragements and successes Affiliation with the state and national association brings an enlarged outlook, one beyond the confines of the local community to the larger interest of all children, enabling the local association to work toward the solution of local problems in the light of the relation of those problems to a general scheme of child welfare Considered from the larger viewpoint, no local association can do its full duty by its own children unless it feels that it is contributing somewhat to better conditions for all children Only by joining its forces with other similar forces as in a state and national association can this purpose be realized

The state and national associations offer certain definite helps to local associations The state and national year books give many concrete, helpful suggestions, speakers are often furnished for expenses, and suggestions for programs are given loan papers on many phases of child welfare may be secured from the national association outlines of community work and advice as to undertakings are given, and the national and state meetings afford opportunity for information and conferences on subjects especially vital to parent-teacher associations as well as inspiration for renewed effort The efficiency of such assistance as this depends upon a large membership in the state and national association

TYPES OF SCHOOLS

Parent-teacher associations may be successfully organized in connection with all types of schools, the one-room country school, the consolidated township school, the village school of two or more rooms, the poor district city school, the good district city school, the suburban school, the kindergarten, the primary school, the grammar school, and the high school While the lines of study and the undertakings to be initiated may differ in these various types of associations the problems in all are the problems of the home and school, the underlying purpose is the same and the same form of organization and methods of work may be used

HIGH SCHOOL PARENT-TEACHER ASSOCIATIONS

While many communities see the importance of a parent-teacher association organized in connection with the primary and grammar school and even the kindergarten, they have been slow to appreciate its value in the high school. And yet in the high school such associations are oftentimes most needed, and oftentimes of the greatest service. It is true that many of the individual problems are different from those of the grades and require a different treatment and a somewhat different point of view. But at no time in the child's life is it more important that the home and school cooperate in his training and that parents agree among themselves and unite with teachers on policies and standards of conduct. It is at this age that some of the most difficult problems of youth arise. When the children reach the high school they begin to have more and more interests outside the home, and they begin to come more and more under the influences outside both the home and the school. They begin to feel that spirit of independence that makes them want to be responsible for their own conduct and more impatient of accepting standards from others.

A real cooperation among all parents of the community and with the teachers, a real understanding by parents and teachers of the problems of adolescence and the problems of the home and the school in dealing with young people, and a sympathetic attitude toward these problems can do much to tide children safely thru this period in their lives. Impatient criticism of the schools of today by parents comfortably sitting by their own firesides, idle complaints by teachers of the incompetence of the modern parent, and futile comparisons of the imperfections of the youth of today with the perfections of that of a quarter of a century ago do not help.

Parents and teachers need to understand the problems thoroly and then face them fairly and squarely. Such matters as social activities of the high school pupils, the practice of chaperonage of social affairs, the evening on which such affairs should be held, home study, school spirit, leisure-time activities, athletics, scholarship, dress, debates, dramatics, and many other concrete problems are all problems which parents and teachers need to work out together. It must not be forgotten that before initiating any undertaking or engaging in any activity a thoro knowledge of conditions is necessary. It is highly desirable that a brief general survey of the high school should be made by committees of the parent-teacher association and the facts made known to the entire membership at the beginning of the year. Suggestions for the form and subjects to be included in the survey are given in the Appendix in a survey of high school life and conditions made by the parent-teacher association of the Fort Wayne (Indiana) high school.

RURAL PARENT-TEACHER ASSOCIATIONS

Special attention should be paid to the organization of parent-teacher associations in connection with rural schools. While the need for parent-teacher associations in rural communities is often greater than in town or city communities it is likely to be less apparent. In the denser populations of towns and cities, social problems appear to be closer at hand and more pressing, the need for organized effort in their solution is more easily recognized, and the habit of coöperative work already developed in towns and cities makes it easier to organize parent-teacher associations. In most country districts social problems are not so clearly seen, the habit of coöperative effort has not been so highly developed, and, while members of country communities are not less interested in the training and general welfare of their children, distance from the school, often poor roads, inertia, regular routine and long hours on the farm combine to make it harder to organize parent-teacher associations. These very considerations make it more important even than in towns and cities that homes be brought to the school.

The reasons for bringing the school to the homes in rural districts are even more striking. The teacher in the country school is very often a girl

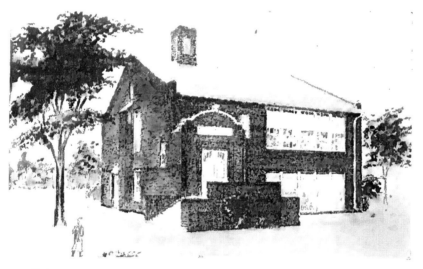

SCHOOL DISTRICT NO. 1, RAMSEY COUNTY, MINNESOTA.
Arthur S. Devor, Architect, St. Paul, 1919.

brought up in a town or city with practically no knowledge, understanding, or sympathy with the life and problems of country children. She often comes to the school on Monday morning of each week and leaves on Friday afternoon, living a life entirely apart from that of the community in which the school is located. It is often difficult for parents and teachers in such a community to discover any common human interest, but the parent-teacher association should help the teacher to catch the spirit of the community, should help the parents to lay aside their embarrassment and diffidence sufficiently to take advantage of the things which the teacher can bring from the outside, and help both to find a common ground for service to the children of the school.

It is highly important that a strong leader be found to head the organi-zation of a rural association, and that this leader be an established member of the community. No community is so scattered and unorganized but that it can at once select one or two such leaders and no community so backward but that it can develop others. The county superintendent of schools and the local trustee can help very materially in the organization of such an association.

School needs and problems of the children of school age in the school and home are much the same everywhere and rural associations will properly consider many of the very same problems of the town and city associations. Some of these problems will be found to be of a more pressing nature in rural districts than in towns and cities. For example, the sanitation of the country school building is in many cases much more difficult than in the more densely populated district of the city or town. The water supply in itself is a difficult matter. In towns and cities the purity of the water is usually a municipal matter, and responsibility for such is not placed on the school authorities alone. But in country districts the water supply most usually comes from individual wells and cisterns, always a potential source of disease, and the school authorities alone must take the responsibility to see that it is pure. The social life of the children in the school is an example of another type of problem often more acute in the country districts than in towns and cities where there are usually a number of carefully organized facilities to furnish entertainment and guide the social life of the children. Thus, while the problems may be essentially the same in both types of associations, they are often more acute in the rural districts.

Rural communities may find it especially desirable to develop the social center idea in connection with their parent-teacher association. They may want to emphasize the informational and entertainment side of their meetings. Outside speakers for lectures on subjects of general interest may be secured for one or two meetings of the year. There may be an occasional musical or literary program. The social and intellectual side of country life is so often entirely neglected that young people are driven to the towns and cities, and rural life becomes more and more depressing. The parent-teacher association in such a district may well become a nucleus for the formation of various types of community clubs especially adapted to country life. Canning clubs, gardening clubs, farming clubs and contests in corn growing, potato raising, tomato clubs, bread baking, stock and grain judging may be organized by the parent-teacher association.

SUCCESSFUL PARENT-TEACHER ASSOCIATIONS

Out of the experience of the past have been found certain things that contribute to the success of any parent-teacher association. The personality of the leader has very much to do with such success. The true leader is marked by real qualities of leadership: a desire to work and not to complain of each task as an additional burden; a desire to give real thought to the problems and not treat them in a light, frivolous manner; a willingness to forget self, to acknowledge mistakes and not to sound his own praises; a belief in the importance of the work, courage to speak out and to brave criticism in carrying on the work; kindness and courtesy to all, tolerance of the opinions of others, reliability, the power to inspire others to work, some experience and first hand knowledge of life, either a knowledge of home, school, and community problems or the ability and industry to acquire such knowledge, good judgment which will not be swept away by some sensational or sentimental argument but which proceeds upon a thoro knowledge of all the phases involved in a problem, and an adherence to common-sense methods in dealing with every subject as it arises No person should be put in office simply because of money or social prominence

The meetings of the most successful parent-teacher associations are conducted according to parliamentary law with due observance of punctuality in opening and closing, and concise, crisp conduct of the business The programs should be practical and helpful While it is desirable to have an occasional outside speaker for an inspirational address, it is better most of the time to have the discussion type of meeting—addresses or papers short and to the point, with questions and full discussions in which all take part No subjects except those related directly to the welfare of children should be allowed Political, religious, and class discussions should be barred That association which is dominated by factional politics, fanatics, or faddists or which is made a tool for furthering personal ambition, or an outlet for church or neighborhood rivalry is doomed to failure The successful parent-teacher association knows no church, no politics, no class, no nationality, but is a place where all may unite for real cooperative work Entertainment features may be included in the meetings, but they should not be allowed to become the chief interest of the meetings Meetings should be held at the schoolhouse.

In order to be successful the parent-teacher association not only holds meetings once a month but initiates some specific undertakings These undertakings should not be scattered over a wide field or be too many But a few definite things should be determined upon, and the responsibility for carrying these out distributed as widely as possible over a number of committees These committees should be wisely chosen, instructed carefully, and held responsible for their respective tasks This gives the association a definite motive without which it is likely to die for lack of interest.

It must not be forgotten that the parent-teacher association belongs equally to parents and teachers both so far as privileges in the association are concerned and responsibility for carrying on the work Parents and teachers should both share in the benefits of the association and the burden of the work should be equally divided And in this connection it must not be forgotten that half of the parents are fathers

Whether or not the finances of the association shall be raised by individual dues or otherwise is a matter for the local association to decide In some communities a moderate amount of dues means an increased interest on the part of the membership, on the theory that where there is money invested there is an increased obligation In other communities the assessment of dues means the shutting out of some of the very parents who would be most benefited by the association and who could contribute most to its success

The successful parent-teacher association has a viewpoint large enough to see beyond the confines of the local community Any outside contacts contribute to this broader vision Usually affiliation with the state and national associations enlarges the viewpoint

The successful parent-teacher association tries to assume neither the responsibilities nor the functions of the school authorities, but works with them for the benefit of children. The parent-teacher association should not assume the burden of raising money for equipment or carrying on activities that properly belong to the school authorities. It is perfectly proper, however, for such associations to step into the breach to furnish equipment or raise money to carry on certain school activities until public sentiment can be created, and the taxpayers brought to see that these are proper school functions to be supported by public taxation.

THE GIANT STRIDE

The successful parent-teacher association does not attempt to supplant the school authorities in matters of school administration and academic work. Teachers and superintendents in the past feared hostile criticism and meddlesome interference with the affairs of the school. The chief concern of the parent-teacher association should be to prevent this very thing and to create an understanding and appreciation of the efforts of the school to the end that their efficiency may be greatly increased. In the earlier days this very matter was the rock on which many parent-teacher associations were wrecked, but specific instructions from the state and national associations have brought about a much better state of affairs.

History of the Movement and the National Organization

HISTORY OF PARENT-TEACHER ASSOCIATIONS

PARENT-teacher association work is one department of work of the National Congress of Mothers and Parent-Teacher Associations In its efforts for child welfare the Congress of Mothers early came to the conclusion that since the home is the greatest factor in child welfare, some practical plan must be thought out for reaching every home with its organization The scheme of organizing parents and teachers in connection with every school was decided upon as the most practical way to reach every home in the country because of the nation-wide extent and thoro organization of the school system, and because the school is the one institution which touches practically every home in the community It is the ultimate aim of the Congress of Mothers to make the organization of parent-teacher associations co-extensive with the school system

In 1907 the department of parent-teacher associations was therefore created in the National Congress of Mothers to promote the organization of such associations thruout the United States In 1908 the name of the National Congress of Mothers was changed to the National Congress of Mothers and Parent-Teacher Associations, the addition being made because it was found that the constituency of the national organization was largely made up of parent-teacher associations, and also because the Congress of Mothers wanted to make it clearly understood that fathers and teachers are welcome in the membership of the organization

The Congress of Mothers and Parent-Teacher Associations stands as the mother body of parent-teacher associations and the history of the parent-teacher movement is bound up in that of the National Congress of Mothers and Parent-Teacher Associations Because of this relationship certain facts about the Mothers Congress are here presented

HISTORY OF THE NATIONAL ORGANIZATION

The National Congress of Mothers and Parent-Teacher Associations was founded at Washington, D C, February 17 1897, by Mrs. Theodore W. Birney and Mrs Phoebe A Hearst. Mrs Birney, herself a mother of children, was struck by the fact that nowhere was there a place to look for instruction in methods of bringing up children She conceived the idea of a national organization which might serve this purpose She talked over the matter with Mrs Phoebe A Hearst and together they worked for months on a plan for organization and preparations for a national meeting for organizing The meeting was called for February 17, 1897, and several hundred men and women fathers and mothers, persons engaged in philanthropy, religion education social affairs government affairs, and members of the press—met in Washington and formed the National Congress of Mothers

The Congress was originally incorporated for forty years, but in 1915 was incorporated in perpetuity in order that bequests to the endowment fund might be legally received

There have been two presidents of the Congress of Mothers: Mrs Theodore W Birney who served from 1897 to 1902, and Mrs Frederic K Schoff, the present president who has served since 1902

Organization. For carrying out the purposes of the Congress it is organized nationally, by state branches and by local organizations There are now recognized branches in thirty six states, and three other states are organized, but not as state branches The following states have state branches Alabama, Arizona California, Connecticut, Colorado, Delaware, District of Columbia, Georgia, Idaho, Illinois Indiana Iowa, Kansas Kentucky, Maine, Maryland, Massachusetts, Michigan, Mississippi, Missouri, Montana, North Carolina, New Hampshire, New York, Ohio, Oregon, Pennsylvania, Rhode Island, South Dakota Tennessee, Texas, Utah, Vermont, Washington, Wisconsin and Wyoming The three states with only local associations are Florida, New Mexico and South Carolina

To the state branches are delegated certain powers and duties by the National Congress the carrying forward of all branches of work of the National Congress, the formation of county branches, the appointment of state chairmen of all departments authorized by the National Congress, oversight and suggestion to all department chairmen as to their duties in carrying out their work in local associations and in reporting to the National Congress, and as a member of the national board a share in forming the policy of the National Congress in its work

County and city councils of parent-teacher associations are authorized by the National Congress of Mothers

Aside from the great number of local parent-teacher associations there are local mothers' circles pre-school circles, parents' associations in churches and child welfare circles affiliated with the Congress

The National Congress is organized for work in the following departments and committees: Americanization, better films, children's books, child hygiene, child welfare day, child labor, child welfare legislation, committee on federal legislation, country life, child welfare magazine education endowment fund, home economics, home and school gardens, home education division, juvenile court and probation, kindergarten extension, loan papers on child nurture marriage sanctity membership mothers' circles national organizer, obstetrics, parents' associations in churches, parent-teacher associations, press and publicity social extension, thrift, and coordination The chairmen of these various departments and the committees are to direct state department chairmen of like departments

NATIONAL CONVENTION

A national convention is held each year by the National Congress Twenty-four annual conventions and three international congresses have so far been held nine in Washington, D C, and one in each of the following

cities Des Moines, Iowa , Columbus, Ohio , Chicago Ill , Detroit, Mich ,
Los Angeles, Calif ; New Orleans La   Denver, Colo , St Louis, Mo ,
Boston, Mass , Portland, Ore , Nashville Tenn   Atlantic City N J ,
Kansas City, Mo , and Madison, Wis   All members of the state and
national associations may attend the convention, join in discussions, and
enjoy the events of the convention   Delegates having voting privileges are
chosen by each state   The president, treasurer, recording secretary, and
corresponding secretary of the state association or their representatives
are voting delegates, and each state is allowed other delegates on the basis
of one delegate (and one alternate) for every five hundred members as
shown in the books of the national treasurer

MEMBERSHIP IN THE NATIONAL CONGRESS OF MOTHERS

There are four types of membership   active, associate, sustaining, and
life   Active membership in a local association affiliated with the state
and national organization carries with it membership in the state and
national organizations. The dues for such membership are 10 cents, half
of which is retained by the state association and half forwarded to the
national association   There are at the present time about 200,000 active
members

Associate memberships may be taken for $1 half of which is retained
by the state association and half forwarded to the national association ,
sustaining memberships for $10 or more yearly, all of which goes to the
national treasury, and life memberships of $50, all of which goes to the
national treasury   Each state fixes the sum for its own sustaining and
life memberships

FOUNDERS' DAY

At the annual convention of 1910 it was voted to celebrate founders'
day each year, on February 17 with a special program   On this day
there is given an account of the founding of the Congress, a message from
the national chairman of the founders' day department, a resumé of the
results accomplished by the association, and a birthday offering is taken
for the national association

FINANCIAL SUPPORT

The national organization is supported by dues paid in by local associations by dues from other types of memberships, by offerings by the
local associations and by gifts   This money is used to support the national
office in Washington to secure clerical help supplies of stationery and
postage, equipment, typewriters mimeograph machines filing cases, printing, to pay for supplies of educational and explanatory literature, for the
support of the *Child Welfare Magazine*, expenses of organization, traveling
expenses, and the expense of the annual convention

THE CHILD WELFARE MAGAZINE

The *Child Welfare Magazine* is the official organ of the Congress   In
1901 the magazine was started as a quarterly with Mrs R R Cotton as

editor It was given up in two years because of the expense In 1906 it was again started as the *National Congress of Mothers' Magazine* with Mrs Howard W Lippincott as the national chairman of the magazine committee In 1908, Mrs Howard W Lippincott, Mrs Frederic Schoff Mrs D O Mears, and Mrs J P Mumford arranged for the organization and incorporation of the Child Welfare Company for the publication of the magazine The company was incorporated with $15,000 capital stock at $10 per share, the Congress of Mothers to control the stock The name of the magazine was changed to the *Child Welfare Magazine*

Subscriptions to the magazine are $1 a year or 75 cents in clubs of five or more New associations paying dues of $5 or more are entitled to one copy of the magazine for one year free provided they send in a list of the names and addresses of their officers and members and their receipt from the state treasurer showing that they have paid their dues and what amount, to the Child Welfare Company, P O. Box 1022 West Philadelphia

COOPERATIVE ARRANGEMENTS WITH NATIONAL ORGANIZATIONS

Since 1913 the National Congress of Mothers has held a conference with the Department of Superintendence of the National Education Association each year at their annual meeting The programs of this conference are printed by the National Education Association These conferences afford an opportunity to bring the work and purposes of the National Congress of Mothers directly before school superintendents and other leaders in education and to secure their cooperation

In 1913 the U S Bureau of Education opened the Home Education Division with Mrs Frederic K Schoff, president of the National Congress of Mothers and Parent-Teacher Associations, as director Mrs. Schoff gave her services to the division free Miss Ellen C Lombard was secured as secretary and her salary was paid by the National Congress of Mothers for several years On account of a new federal law this arrangement with the Bureau of Education became impossible In 1919, the U S Congress failed to make specific appropriation for the support of the Home Education Division in the U S Bureau of Education but arrangements have now been made to utilize the resources of the universities of the country to continue the work * (For description of the arrangement in Indiana see p 30) The Home Education Division was established to direct parents in continuing their education by recommending reading courses on subjects of a general nature and especially on the care and training of children Special reading courses for boys and girls are offered Literature of the Congress of Mothers is used by the division and encouragement is given for the organization of parent-teacher associations in schools

The National Congress of Mothers also cooperates with the U S Department of Agriculture, the Federal Children's Bureau, the U.S Treasury Department in its thrift and savings division For a number of years it has worked with the International Kindergarten Union

---

* The Indiana University Extension Division was the first to put into effect the plan of cooperation in the Home Reading work

The Indiana Parent-Teacher Association

HISTORY

THE Indiana Parent-Teacher Association, a branch of the National Congress of Mothers and Parent-Teacher Associations, was organized June 7, 1912. A group of Indiana women who attended the convention of the National Congress of Mothers and Parent-Teacher Associations at St Louis in March invited Mrs Frederic Schoff to come to Indianapolis on her way home to talk over the matter of organizing an Indiana branch of that organization. This meeting was held at the Y W C A. on March 28 with Mrs Schoff and Mrs Orville T Bright and a committee was appointed to call a state meeting. The state meeting was called June 7, 1912. Mrs Bright, representing the National Congress of Mothers, took charge of the business session, and the Indiana branch was formally organized as the Indiana Congress of Mothers and Parent-Teacher Associations, with Mrs Fred Hoke of Indianapolis as president.

In October 1919 the name of the state organization was changed and it was incorporated for fifty years as the Indiana Parent-Teacher Association.

The state association is organized to strengthen and unify local parent-teacher associations and acts as a bureau of information and help to these and other organizations working for the welfare of children in school and home.

Organization. The officers of the state association are a president, a vice-president-at-large, a vice-president from each of the thirteen congressional districts of the state, executive secretary, recording secretary, and auditor. These officers (with the exception of the executive secretary) are elected every two years at an annual convention. These officers are members of the state executive board. Honorary vice-presidents may be elected by reason of distinguished service to the state association.

An advisory council of from ten to fifteen members is elected every two years by the state executive board to meet at the call of the state president to advise with the association in regard to its affairs.

The state executive board is composed of the officers of the state association, the presidents of the districts, the presidents of the counties, the president of the board of department chairmen and six members elected every two years. This board meets regularly twice each year, once just before and once just after the state convention. It also meets on call of the president when needed.

For working purposes the state association is organized by departments and committees corresponding to those of the National Congress of Mothers and Parent-Teacher Associations. The chairman of each state department is a member of the corresponding committee in the national organization. The following departments are organized in the state association. Americanization, better films, child hygiene, country life, founders' day, education to include home and school gardens, home economics and thrift, juvenile courts and probation, kindergarten extension, legislation to include child labor, child welfare, and federal legislation, press and publicity, mothers' pensions, recreation, social extension including the community center idea, and state organizer. The powers and duties of the following departments of the National Congress have not been delegated to departments, but are retained by the governing body of the state association: children's books, child welfare magazine, membership promotion, parent-teacher associations coordination. The state organization has no departments of marriage sanctity, endowment fund, loan papers on child nurture, mothers' circles, obstetrics, and parents' associations in churches.

The chairmen of the departments are appointed annually by the executive board. Together they form the board of department chairmen which elects officers every two years at the state convention. Their president is a member of the state executive board.

The state association is organized according to districts, counties, cities, and local associations.

The state is divided according to the thirteen congressional districts and each district is organized with a president who acts as vice-president of the state association and is a member of the state executive board. These presidents are appointed by the state executive board until there are enough counties organized in the district to elect their own officers. Meetings may be called in the district by the state president or that officer's representative.

Counties and Cities. The districts are organized according to counties, with a president for each county appointed by the executive board until counties have enough parent-teacher associations affiliated with the state association to organize county councils. In any county where there are three or more parent-teacher associations county councils may be formed. The meeting to form such a council in any county is called by the state president or the representative of the state president. The officers of the county council are a president, a vice-president, secretary, and treasurer to be elected each year at a regular meeting of the council. Membership in the county council consists of the membership of the local parent-teacher associations forming the council, but the voting members are the officers of the county council, the township chairmen, and the president, secretary, and one delegate for every ten paid members of each local parent-teacher association forming the council. The presidents of the counties are members of the state executive boards. Each county is in turn divided into townships with a chairman for each township.

City councils similar to the county councils may be organized in cities where there are three or more parent-teacher associations affiliated with the state association. These councils are organized by the county president or the representative of the county president. (For suggested constitutions for county and city councils see Appendix.)

ANNUAL CONVENTION

The state association holds an annual convention which since 1919 is held at the time and place of the Indiana State Teachers' Association Members of local affiliated associations have all the privileges of the convention except that of voting, a privilege which belongs to delegates only Each affiliated association may send to the convention as delegates its president and one delegate for every ten paid members The program for these conventions is made out by the state executive board with the help of any members whom it wants to call in to act with it on this matter Annual conventions have been held since 1912 in Huntington in 1913, Lafayette, 1914, Indianapolis, 1915, Evansville, 1916, Fort Wayne, 1917 and 1918; and Indianapolis, 1919

MEMBERSHIP AND AFFILIATED ASSOCIATIONS

Membership in the Indiana Parent-Teacher Association is of six kinds honorary, active, associate, state sustaining, state benefactors, and state life members

Parent-teacher associations organized in connection with the schools, and certain other child welfare organizations which are approved by the state executive board are eligible to membership in the state association on the payment of dues of 10 cents a member for organizations of 50 or less and a flat rate of $5 for organizations of 50 or more Half of the dues are retained in the state treasury and half forwarded to the National Congress All the members of such are considered active members of the state association, but only such a number as have been paid for at the rate of 10 cents a member can be members of the National Congress of Mothers and Parent-Teacher Associations There are at this time 113 local associations in Indiana affiliated with the state and national organizations This represents a total membership of about 10,000 in the state association, 5,800 of which are entitled to membership in both state and national associations by reason of having been paid for at the rate of 10 cents a member.

Other educational organizations not organized as parent-teacher associations but desiring to cooperate in the work of the Indiana Parent-Teacher Association, if approved by the state executive board, may be affiliated upon payment of $3 dues half of which is retained in the state treasury and half forwarded to the National Congress of Mothers

The state superintendent of public instruction, the county superintendents of schools, and the superintendents of city schools in the state are considered honorary members Associate memberships may be secured on payment of $1 yearly half of which is retained by the state treasury and half of which is forwarded to the National Congress of Mothers State sustaining memberships may be secured on payment of $5 annually, state benefactors, $50 at the time of taking the membership and state life membership, $25 at the time of taking the membership

STATE ORGANIZER

The power of organizing local parent-teacher associations has not been specifically delegated to a state organizer The state president as the executive officer of the association acts in this capacity or designates certain individuals to act for her. District and county presidents, acting for the president, do a great deal of organizing work in their local districts and counties.

Various devices are employed to promote interest among teachers and educators in organizing. Speakers present the matter to county institutes, to local teachers' meetings, and to various state meetings. Propaganda is carried on by letters, pamphlets, and personal interviews. Requests from local groups for help in organizing are answered in so far as possible by the state association. Interest in parent-teacher associations in high schools has been greatly stimulated by the stipulation in the classification of the high schools of the state that in order to be put in class A the high school must have a parent-teacher association affiliated with the state association.

FINANCIAL SUPPORT

The association is supported by the dues from local associations, from associate memberships half of which are retained in the state treasury and half forwarded to the National Treasury, by dues from state sustaining memberships, state life memberships, and state benefactors, all of which are retained in the state treasury, and by gifts from individuals and from local associations. Very material assistance such as printing, clerical help, etc., is also given by various state and private organizations with which the association cooperates.

This money is used to cover the expenses of the state convention, postage and stationery used by the association, the printing of leaflets and pamphlets, and the general running expenses of the association.

MONTHLY BULLETIN

Since January, 1920 the association has sent out monthly a mimeographed bulletin during the winter months with notices, items of interest, plans of work, etc., to local associations affiliated with it. This bulletin is the official organ of the state association and together with the state convention and personal communications affords the means of direct contact between the state association and local associations affiliated with it.

ACTIVITIES OF THE ASSOCIATION

For the year 1919-20 the state association suggested the following lines of work to local associations affiliated with it: health—the modern health crusade, health talks in the schools, clinics—especially dental clinics—scales in every school, school attendance, especially in the rural schools, and thrift in cooperation with the thrift activities of the federal government. In addition to these activities the association has cooperated with the Indiana Child Welfare Association in its plans, has taken an active part in the "Teacher Week in Indiana" campaign, has given its active support to the following bills in the U S Congress—the Smith-Towner education bill, the Shepperd-Towner maternity and infancy protection bill, and the Fess bill for the promotion of physical education; has urged its local associations to establish systems of school feeding, and has cooperated with the Indiana Indorsers of Photo-Plays in an attempt to bring about a demand by the public for better moving pictures and to secure good pictures from the producers

For the year 1920-21 the state association suggests the following lines of interest to its local associations health—modern health crusade, health supervision in public schools health laws, recreation and physical education school lunches lectures on child hygiene sanitary conditions of school buildings and grounds, scales in every school, courses in general biology in schools to solve problems in sex education school nurses and all-time health officers, school attendance—a study of the problem, an attempt to keep children in school without using the force of the law, thrift—a study of thrift principles teaching of thrift, cooperation with the thrift program of the United States government Other suggested subjects for study or activity are the following the community center national holidays, juvenile delinquency beautification of school grounds, music in the schools, books and pictures in the schools, kindergartens and primary work, Americanization, moving pictures rural schools, and teachers salaries

COOPERATIVE ARRANGEMENT WITH THE EXTENSION DIVISION OF INDIANA UNIVERSITY

In October, 1919 the Extension Division of Indiana University opened a Bureau of Parent-Teacher Associations to give more direct service to all parent-teacher associations of the state The Indiana Parent-Teacher Association functions thru this bureau State headquarters of the association are in the Extension Division and a member of its staff acts as executive secretary of the association Materials of the association are kept in the Extension Division files and clerical help is given by the division

Pamphlets, leaflets, and letters on various phases of the welfare of children and printed matter of the association are distributed by the division, using postage of the association A mimeographed bulletin is sent each month from the division to local associations affiliated with the state association The Extension Division acts in an advisory capacity to the association on questions of general policy and specific undertakings Advisory service is also given local associations

HOME READING COURSES IN THE EXTENSION DIVISION OF INDIANA UNIVERSITY

The Extension Division of Indiana University has taken over the management for Indiana of the Home Reading courses of the United States Bureau of Education When the U S. Congress failed to appropriate sufficient money for the support of the Home Education Division in the United States Bureau of Education at Washington, arrangement was made to utilize the resources of the universities Indiana University was the first to effect a plan of cooperation with Commissioner Claxton and put it into operation Accordingly, the Home Reading Courses for the National Reading Circle of the United States Bureau of Education are being continued The work of distributing the courses and assisting readers in Indiana is done by the Extension Division of Indiana University. Parent-teacher associations may continue this work in cooperation with Indiana University.

COÖPERATION WITH THE INDIANA CHILD WELFARE ASSOCIATION

The Indiana Parent-Teacher Association is one of a number of organizations which have associated themselves together to form the Indiana Child Welfare Association. This organization is a state-wide organization of representatives of public and private, state and national agencies doing child welfare work in Indiana, of individuals interested in child welfare, and of child welfare committees in the various counties of the state. It is a cooperative association to work for the realization of a complete program of child care in Indiana.

COOPERATION WITH THE INDIANA STATE TEACHERS' ASSOCIATION

In November, 1919, the Indiana Parent-Teacher Association was made a regular section of the Indiana State Teachers' Association. The annual meeting of the state Parent-Teacher Association is held at the same time and place as the State Teachers' Association and its programs are arranged with and printed by the State Teachers' Association along with the general program of that body.

Papers Read at the State Convention of the Indiana Parent-Teacher Association, November, 1919

ANNUAL ADDRESS OF THE PRESIDENT

Mrs. Hence Orme

Once again we meet in our annual convention This year the dark war cloud has lifted, but the effects of war have not been effaced War has left its stamp upon us, and many years will come and go before we have forgotten war s grim chances The adult population of America did not suffer very much We were asked to save and conserve, and we did, with little or no inconvenience to us, but the children of America were overlooked for a time

We went into Red Cross work and other war activities with such vim that we overlooked some of the most important things, and the one which above all others we should have stopped to consider was the welfare of the children

This oversight was not intentional on our part, but the task of getting our army equipped was seemingly the one thing upon which we should bend all efforts for the time, and when we did get a consciousness on the matter things had gone too far First, there had been a general upheaval of affairs, all regular processes of life had been broken up, second, a general let-down along moral and social lines third, a general hardening of the imagination, a natural sequence of war. fourth, mothers and older children had been compelled to go into factory and munition plants to work The result of these four things, when it became evident to us, was appalling Juvenile courts were full of our little ones, young girls barely entered into womanhood were mothers of illegitimate children, and sex improprieties were a common thing, especially in districts where there were camps and cantonments False standards of living had been set up, and our national ideals were threatened England sent us words of warning, and we were wise enough to heed them

The first thing we did was to take stock of ourselves and we found that we were lacking in the care of the child The Children s Bureau in Washington immediately sent out a call for a whole year to be devoted to the study and work for the child. Every child was to be weighed and measured, and a hundred thousand babies were to be saved This, however, we cannot say was done, and this was the weakest point in the program for Children s Year However much good was accomplished for the welfare of the child was made a community responsibility and the educational value of Children's Year can never be estimated

Much of the work of this year was done by the Parent-Teacher Association We threw our forces into the field with all vigor and accepted responsibility for certain parts of the state This organization eight years old in the state, is a part of the National Congress of Mothers and Parent-Teacher Associations. With twenty-five years of work for the child behind us in the national, and eight years' experience in the state, we feel that we can come to the intelligent citizenship of this state with a program that will arouse their interest and sympathy.

The first point in our program is health. There are several things essential to health: good food, exercise, sensible clothing, and plenty of fresh air. We must continue to talk school lunches and the warm lunch at noon. This must be a part of our work until every child is cared for in that respect. The Extension Division of Indiana University has recently issued a very good bulletin on 'Feeding Children at School.' It is free for the asking.

Recreation is necessary for the growth of the child in order that the body may function properly. Physical education should be a part of every school curriculum, not a side-issue. Our last legislature passed a law giving to school children, in cities of 5,000 or more, physical education, forgetting that the majority of the children in our public schools do not live in cities of 5,000. What does the state intend to do for the remainder of the school children of this state? I fear that lawmakers are not only ignorant of modern methods of child welfare, but absolutely indifferent to anything but their own selfish political interests. The greatest thing in Indiana is not the political issue of either party, not the tax commission, not the industrial conditions, tho they all affect the body as a whole, but the greatest thing in our great commonwealth today is the welfare of our 600,000 school children, and our 200,000 little ones under school age. And Indiana as a state has failed miserably in her duty if any little child is deprived of any opportunity of development.

Health must ever be a paramount issue as regards the child life of our state. We are wasting money when we attempt to educate sickly children. There are in the United States today 20,000,000 school children, fully 15,000,000 of whom are defective physically. It is safe to say that Indiana has among her 600,000 school children her share of defectives, witness 700 mentally deficient in the School for Feeble-Minded at Fort Wayne.

Those who have made a study of this matter tell us that much of the physical defectiveness comes from malnutrition, and a large per cent of malnutrition comes from bad teeth. We must have in this state a mandatory medical inspection law for our public schools. Every child must be examined and then compelled to have his defect or disease treated before he can again be a pupil in our schools.

We need a new health law in this state. Under the present system or machine, which was put into force in 1881, and consequently very much antiquated, we have 550 health officers in the state. Most of them object to a change in the law, and the reason is obvious. They draw public money and do not render the equivalent. Hence they are not willing for a change.

Under this system or machine we do not have trained men in office. Appointments are made because of political pull, and the health officer does not give full time to the duties of his office. Under a new system we would have men giving full time to the work, men trained for that purpose, and they would be unobstructed by fear of losing office because of displeasing a patron since his reputation does not depend upon that side of his professional life. He will give service and be diligent and faithful in performance of his duties.

The visiting health nurse is needed in every county in this state, and public health demands that, especially in rural Indiana, we have these nurses going about rendering a very much needed service. With the all-time health officer and the visiting health nurse, Indiana will soon be at the top in Child Welfare.

A short time ago, a survey was made of 10,000 country and city children. The city children were found to be in far better health than those from the country. Typhoid fever in rural Indiana was 2 per cent on the increase above the urban communities. In Indiana every year we spend $20,000,000 on sickness, disease, and death, and each year we buy 23,000 short coffins, a great economic and spiritual loss to our state. Little ones are uncared for who might, if they had proper treatment and care, grow into useful citizens.

These are grave questions and should be considered from the standpoint of service to humanity, and every parent-teacher association in the state can do its share toward arousing public sentiment for these health laws.

Another task that confronts us is getting and keeping every boy and girl of school age in school. We must make parents understand that an educated, trained mind will mean more to them and to the child in the industrial world than the puny efforts of the untrained, uneducated boy or girl now. A few years of waiting until the child has been trained to work efficiently will mean much both to the state and to the individual. At the suggestion of your president the state board of truancy issued a pamphlet on the school attendance law, and you may have this by writing to Mr. Amos Butler, Statehouse.

We believe in the child, and we believe it is good for him to work, and we would under no circumstances endorse a prohibitive child labor law. Children need to be taught the dignity of work. Often in large cities it is necessary while a child is going to school to open a trades school or class and pay the child for his work, it being done under the supervision of the school and along with other school work. Likewise, it is necessary for the child to have some kind of employment during vacation time, and where there are no vacation schools, then a law that forbids all children to work for pay will work harm rather than good for them. Idle children find their way into juvenile court, hence the need of supervised work during the vacation period. I like the motto of the Junior Republic at Freeville, N.Y., "Nothing without labor." Here in this school the rich and poor work side by side and each must be a productive unit. The result is a better class of skilled workmen and better citizens.

We must eventually have continuation schools like those of Cincinnati and Boston. In Ohio they have a state law authorizing school authorities to establish such schools.

Rural schools of this state must undergo a complete change. No wonder that country boys and girls leave school as soon as they have reached the age limit and often before. School is not attractive and they leave for the workshop and the industrial world, thus depleting the productive force of the state. Education in the rural schools must meet the needs of rural life, and only until such a thing comes to pass in this state will we have the right kind of rural life. We must have vitalized vocational training both in agriculture and domestic science.

We put our children in school at the age of six. They are all poured into the same hopper with no thought of developing initiative, no thought of training the imagination, but each child regardless of his ability is expected to leave school with so much of certain things and we say that they have their elementary education when often they have no education at all. They have gone thru books, they have memorized parts of them, but many are not even able to spell correctly, to say nothing of penmanship. They have not been taught to apply what they have learned to life, and when they leave the schoolroom they often leave what little learning they have received behind them.

Our schools must do certain things: they must teach the child to discover himself, direct himself, sustain himself, hitch education on to life, take hold of the real big problems and make them go.

There are big tasks facing our nation today and we need big men and women to solve them, and we look to the public schools of our land to equip our boys and girls to handle the affairs of men. Unless we can within the next decade turn out of our schools and colleges men and women who can do things and who can get a firm grip on the world our nation is doomed. The hope of the nation lies in the training of the boys and girls in the public schools of today.

Back of the school is the teacher, and no matter how much we need efficient teaching force in this state we will not get it until we pay a wage sufficient for the teacher to live, one that will attract the best men and women to the profession. Higher wages for teachers, increased qualifications must go hand in hand and we, the mothers of the school children of the state must work for those two things.

The third point in our state program is thrift. The government has outlined the plan, and we must fall in with it. If we are able to pay off the tremendous war debt and not leave it to posterity to face our obligations unpaid we must begin to save. War savings and thrift stamps must be bought in great numbers and the children must be trained to save. Write Mrs. Julia Henderson, Hume-Mansur Building, and she will send you helpful material.

My personal contribution to the work the past year has been as follows: letters written, personal, 984, mimeographed letters, 350, packages of literature sent out, 280, postal cards written, 156, addresses made on P. T. A. 79. Practically two-thirds of those organizations which have made state affiliation in the past eleven months have come in because of personal visits on the part of your president or because of letters written.

Your president has called and held two state board meetings, represented the state at two conferences called by our Governor, has served on the state committee of the School Patrons' Committee, a department of the National Educational Association. She has spoken at the annual meeting of the Photo Endorsers of Indiana, has served as vice-chairman of the Woman's Section of the Indiana Roosevelt Memorial Association, as a member of the National Country Life Committee on Rural Education, and a member of the Committee of One Hundred who are endeavoring to make a record in Red Cross Seals sales She has spoken at twenty county teachers' institutes during the past summer and fall, and her only regret in submitting this report is that the days were not longer that she might not have had larger opportunity and more time to work for the children of our state

Recently we have made an affiliation with the Division of Extension of Indiana University with Dr Edna Edmondson, who is in charge of the Child Welfare work of the Division, as the executive secretary of the Indiana Parent-Teacher Association This means more than I can tell you for with such an institution behind us we cannot fail in our purpose Dr Edmondson is admirably fitted for her work, and she brings to us her intense interest in our cause and her love for the child life of our state She is ready at all time to help Write her when you need her advice

Finally dear friends, let us work with renewed energy for our little ones It is a precious heritage we have been given and it is our business to see that every child knows and realizes what the greatest thing in the world is and means, love Our work must be based upon this great principle, and we must be in this work because we love little children, because we see and know its value, and because we realize that, created in image of God it is possible for man to attain that image We must realize that the child does not fail, and that he develops only as we put him in surroundings that are conducive to growth, and that he unfolds his wonderful possibilities at our touch Our reform schools and juvenile courts are a reflection on our homes and we have come to know that the great question with children is not one of charity or correction but one of formation, and for that we are responsible.

All of our modern pedagogy is built around the child and his instincts, and we must bring our lives to conform to the life of the child

We have had for so long our eyes firmly fixed on material progress that we have lost the touch with childhood The play spirit is lost because we have gone too far from the heart of humanity, the child, and we who have felt in our superior adult way that we were teaching the child, and that we really had much to teach him must realize that we have very little after all to reveal to him except the art of growing into adulthood Our children will take us by the hand and lead us into fields Elysian if we will but let them They and they alone can reshape the universe They are the Kingdom Come of mankind, and we must accept the inevitable and live with the children and enter the realm of childhood with the same spirit of confidence that they evidence We talk of children growing up. They never do, but we pull them down to us It is the adult that needs to learn the art of growing up with and to the children No longer is it a boy and girl problem, but a man and woman problem, a mother and father problem Our duty is clear we must hunt up every little child and make his life bright, we must put ourselves on the same level with the children, not on a plane above, we must establish comradeship and good fellowship, and save the little ones for the future

We are being led into a glorious future, today, my friends, because of the little ones and I am sure that there is no one within the hearing of my voice who does not realize this and accept her share of the responsibility of making the world a happier place for the children

Don't blame the government when things go wrong politically, when men so far forget their obligation to humanity as to be dishonest with public funds or to betray a public trust. Blame the homes of this nation, and be sure that disaster cannot befall any nation whose homes are founded upon the great principles of the Divine. No nation can rise above its homes, and the nation that fails in rendering justice toward its children will inevitably suffer.

Big speeches on high ideals will not make the world safe for democracy. We must get into the thickest of the fight for right living and sacrifice ourselves for our ideals. And today if we as a nation and if our leaders had been willing to have done this we should be farther on toward the goal of universal peace than we can ever hope to be when men strive for personal aggrandizement.

The hand of Jehovah has been laid against injustice to little children, and we as mothers and teachers and guardians of the child life of our state and nation must accept the responsibility that is ours and pledge our best efforts, our manhood and womanhood, for the children's cause in Indiana.

AN ADVENTURE IN RURAL HEALTH SERVICE

AMALIA BENGSTON, Superintendent Renville County Schools, Minnesota

When I first became superintendent of the Renville county schools I planned to do all in my power with the money allowed me for the betterment of these schools. I hoped to be able to persuade the people of the county that only the best in schoolhouses, equipment, and teaching force should be thought of for the school children, and with this idea in mind I began visiting schools.

I had made only a few visits, however, when one day I said to myself, "What is the use? What is the use of asking the people of Renville county to spend money in bettering the schools for children who are physically unfit to get the full benefit of what is given them, or for children who are too sick to be in school at all?" For as I went about visiting schools I saw children so badly affected with adenoid and tonsil trouble, children whose eyesight and hearing were so impaired, children who were such victims of malnutrition and nervous disorder that they were unfit physically to get their school work as they should. The more I talked for better schoolhouses and a better teaching force the more convinced I became that I was hitching the cart before the horse. And I saw my duty toward those children in a new light, for I began to realize that an attempt must be made to have medical inspection, and at least give the children an opportunity to be made fit for school as well as make the school fit for the children.

I knew the visiting nurses had done much for the children of the city schools and I reasoned what was good for the city children ought to be good for rural children, were it suited to country conditions, and I began to plan for a county nurse.

To get a nurse would take money, and as I planned to have the health work paid for by county money appropriated by the county board of commissioners, I knew that I must work up some sentiment for our proposed health work among the taxpayers before the commissioners would feel justified in giving me an appropriation My first move therefore was a campaign for public sentiment

At every meeting where I had an opportunity to speak I took occasion to tell of health conditions among the school children as I had observed them I pointed out what the cities had done for their school children for some years past and how conditions had been bettered I argued that the people of prosperous Renville county ought to give this health question some consideration Some one or two in every gathering would come to me at the close of such a meeting, say they were interested and ask what I proposed to do To these I explained my plan for a county nurse, and asked that those interested would take occasion to speak with their county commissioner, asking him to give me at least thoughtful attention when I brought the subject up at a meeting of the board When enough people seemed interested, I went before the county commissioners and asked for an appropriation for our health campaign, if nothing more, enough money so that we could "try out" our plan

The morning I went before the board I did receive the finest kind of attention, for all those men had been interviewed and were more or less ready to express their views and voice all their fears One of these fears was with reference to the legality of the movement, for much to my surprise I found that medical inspection paid for out of public money could only be carried on legally in cities of the first and second class We finally persuaded the commissioners to call the nurse assistant county superintendent (I should like to say here that Minnesota has since passed a mighty fine permissive public health law) and I was given an appropriation of $300, after I guaranteed her traveling expenses out of my own allowance for traveling expenses The most convincing argument used was given by the chairman of the county board, when he said "It paid to have a campaign for better health among the hogs in this county, we might try a little something for the children.' I might add that during two years there was spent, in Renville county, $50,000 to stamp out our epidemic of hog cholera and the farmers all felt it was money well expended

It was the middle of November before our first nurse, Miss Mary Cornish came to us and the work was begun Later Miss Dorothy Motl came

It was the middle of November before we began our work, but from then until Christmas we had good roads and weather so with the use of my Ford we made a good start We worked rapidly examining as many as 89 children a day, and visiting four schools We do not recommend such haste, but in our case it seemed absolutely necessary for we wanted to cover as much of our county as possible in three months and we have 140 schools The children were examined for any symptom of eye, ear, nose, throat, tooth, and skin trouble; in some cases we took temperatures and in others throat culture It was necessary to make many home calls to talk with mothers about their children

Yes, there was opposition to our health work and for the first few weeks we simply had to turn deaf ears to this and work on, trusting that the results would argue for the work Whenever children refused to be examined, saying "My mother said I did not need to be examined by the nurse ' we did not argue with the children, but after we had finished our work in that particular school we made a "home visit", taking the children in question with us. In every case we found it was a matter of misunderstanding and the mother consented to the examination when the work was explained to her. Sometimes children absented themselves from school when they expected the nurse, but they did not escape us, because we made it a point to make a home visit in every case and soon it became noised about that there was no way of escaping the nurse.

Some of my friends said that it was well enough to take a nurse about a county while the weather and roads were good, but when the snow began flying it would be an impossibility to carry on the work. Fate seemed to be with us for, had we set about to demonstrate what could be done under adverse climatic conditions we could have chosen no better winter than we did. For weeks at a time the thermometer played around the 30 below mark and the snow piled in ten- and fifteen-foot drifts, yet we traveled every day that it was at all possible for any human being to be on the roads.

Renville county is prosperous, there are few poor people, no child is underfed, and no one wilfully neglected, yet our tabulated report shows an appalling amount of physical defectiveness. Out of our school population of 6,000 we examined 5,000 and found 4,095 defective, testifying that 81 per cent of the children were defective. This seems almost unbelievable and yet it does not tell the whole story, for I could take you to school after school where there was 100 per cent defectiveness where we sent a notice to the parent of every child in that school. Yet, as I said before Renville county is a prosperous county and we have every reason to believe that conditions found in Renville county today are the same as in other counties where a health survey has been taken. The percentages of the defectiveness found were: teeth, 55 per cent, nose 40 per cent, throat, 66 per cent, eyes, 22 per cent, ears, 17 per cent, malnutrition 16 per cent, nervous disorder, 16 per cent, neck glands, 14 per cent, skin, 13 per cent, and general appearance, 12 per cent.

Think of 17 per cent of our school children being partially deaf, and many of these growing up to face stone deafness unless something were done to correct the trouble while they are still children. And unless some sort of health inspection had been inaugurated nothing would have been done for neither the children nor their parents realized that anything was wrong. We have on record children who were stone deaf in one ear and did not know it, children who had absolutely no sight in one eye and did not know it. Their parents had no realization of the state of affairs, and their teachers had not made the discovery. Who then was to come to the rescue if a nurse had not been employed? Out in our county we know we did not begin the work half soon enough.

The 40 per cent of nose trouble represents the children who were mouth breathers from some cause or other—in a great many cases from adenoids. Children who are mouth breathers, aside from having deformed faces, are a prey to many diseases and almost invariably have throat trouble in addition to their nose trouble. I have here in my hand a plaster of paris mask taken of the face of a fourteen-year-old boy having adenoids (showing mask). Note his short upper lip, his protruding front teeth, the undeveloped nose, and the dead expression under his eyes. To my certain knowledge this fact is typical of a large number of children in our schools. The boy in question had a skilful operation performed and his adenoids removed. He then went to a dentist, a Dr. Miller of Bird Island, in our county, and had his teeth straightened. Here he is eight months later (showing another cast). See what a well-shaped mouth he now has, how his nose has developed, and how his whole face has changed. As I said before, he was only fourteen years old and was growing rapidly hence the marked change in so short a time.

Here is an impression of the mouth of a girl sixteen years old, who had adenoids. Note how the teeth fail to articulate. This girl, while keeping her mouth open in order that she might breathe, had deformed her jaw, and consequently her teeth had grown out of their natural places.

Just a word about malnutrition. According to our report, 689 children in Renville county were apparently underfed. Yet we know these children get all they need to eat, but the fact that they were physically unfit to assimilate properly this food, and consequently showed signs of malnutrition, had escaped the notice of their parents.

Now to ask, "What of it?" "What good came of the health survey?" Our records show that about 1,000 of the children examined were taken to see either a doctor or a dentist or both the first year. Parents who at first opposed the work are fully convinced that a county nurse should be a permanent worker among us, when they see how much their children have benefited by a little medical help.

Besides examining the children, the nurse had been a great factor in bringing about a general education for better health. In our county today you are away behind the times if you do not know what adenoids are and the havoc bad tonsils can bring, why eye-strain is so prevalent and how to prevent it, why teeth should be taken care of, why we should drink plenty of water and eat the proper kind of food, what kind of clothing is best to wear, and why we should not wear too heavy and too much clothing while indoors (we have induced some little boys to remove one coat and three sweaters while in school), why we need to be clean, etc.

Another great service the nurse rendered us was to bring about a veritable epidemic of schoolhouse improvement. She proved that the physical condition of the schoolhouse was reflected in the physical condition of the children, for example, a poorly lighted and badly ventilated schoolhouse always housed children with eye-strain and nervous disorder and in a schoolhouse having ill-fitting desks were children of poor posture.

During the summer of that first year the nurse was with us we conducted so-called "Baby Clinics" in the county, one in every township and one in each village. We urged the mothers to bring the children below school age to the clinics, and much the same kind of an examination was given them as was given to the children of school age. We found that 60 per cent of the children of pre-school age were defective. I am of the conviction that much of our health work should be done with these children of pre-school age so that the glad day will come when children are as physically fit as possible when they enter school.

When the first year's work was completed the question came up as to the employment of a nurse for the second year. By this time there was so much public sentiment for the work that our county board felt justified in appropriating $2,000 for the next year, and now it is no longer a question as to whether or not a nurse should be employed but merely a question as to how much money is to be appropriated

Once in a while someone voices the sentiment that taxes are going up every day, and that expenses must be curtailed, and also once in a while the suggestion comes that the curtailment might be brought about by not employing a nurse but, as happened one day when we proved to one taxpayer that a $2,000 appropriation meant a tax of only 31 cents tax per quarter-section, he is likely to shrug his shoulders and say, 'Oh well, I'd smoke that up in a day or two, and if it's going to help the children any, go ahead."

In short, I believe we have had a new vision that we are thinking less in terms of dollars and cents and more in terms of humanity, I believe we have prayed that prayer of Nellie McClung's and heard its answer

Lord, take us up to the heights, and show us the glory,
Show us a vision of empire! Tell us its story!
Tell it plain, for our eyes and our ears have grown holden
We have forgotten that anything other than money is golden
Grubbing away in the valley somehow has darkened our eyes,
Watching the ground and the crops—we've forgotten the skies,
But, Lord, if thou wilt canst take us today
To the Mount of Decision
And show us the land that we live in
With glorified vision!

FUNDAMENTAL CONCERNS OF THE PARENT-TEACHER ASSOCIATION

L N HINES, State Superintendent of Public Instruction

I am very greatly interested in the proceedings of this association, and in every way I intend to give it all the help of which I am capable I believe in the work of the Parent-Teacher Association, and I believe there are many problems which active intelligent local parent-teacher associations could solve or could help solve

I have two letters in my hand which are typical A woman writes to find out if there is any law to compel the local authorities to repair the schoolhouse She says that practically all the windows are broken There was a hard rain the other day, and a wind blew the rain into the room so that the pupils had to move to the other side Many farmers would hesitate to winter stock in the same quarters, yet our children are forced to attend school in such buildings This woman goes on to say that the stove smokes badly I want to tell you that if this school is a fair sample of some of our country schools, we certainly have room for improvement The woman says that the trustee is uneducated and unfit for the office he is holding, and that she thinks they need an organization of teachers and parents

It is unfortunate that such a man should hold office, but you know how many candidates win office by promising taxpayers that they will have lower taxes They begin where they think there is the least objection and cut expenses there

I have a letter from a farmer who makes this intelligent observation he says that the first thing they need is equipment, and then they need others who realize that a boy and girl mean more to the community than dollars

There is certainly need in this state for an organization in every community to see to it that in every schoolhouse the children are taken care of physically and mentally. Our children are our chief assets in this country As you go around the country you hear that wheat and corn and oats are assets, but I tell you we are rich because we have children We may have these other things and be infinitely poor The crop of children is the biggest crop of all

The parent-teacher program should include better equipment for the schools and better health for the children It is of first importance to do the best possible with the present equipment The school at home may not be what you think it ought to be but do the best you can with what is available, and then continually keep in mind that something better must be had.

Have you parents been to the school? Have you investigated to see whether or not it is kept clean? Have you ever tried to find out whether the schoolrooms are well ventilated? Are the seats comfortable? Are the children interested? Do the children sit in poor light and not complain because they are not conscious of discomfort of any kind? Remember, all this is laying up something that must be paid for in years to come

Is the hearing of the pupil tested? Is correct posture insisted upon? Is work being done along the line of caring for the teeth? And what about the meals at home? There are a lot of things to do, and there are many intelligent teachers to help do it.

When you go home ask your teachers to have a set of compositions written on 'What I Had for Breakfast', and I am sure that any teacher and most parents have something coming in the way of a surprise to see how poorly some children are fed in a number of homes Some breakfasts consist of coffee and pickles Children will not grow into sound manhood and womanhood on coffee and pickles

Is the drinking water in the school safe? In every rural schoolyard there should be a driven well Do the children get enough sleep? Are health habits being taught at school?

Now, I am thoroly in sympathy with the teacher who says that there are too many things in the course of study and she can't undertake these extra jobs But they have to be undertaken by somebody

I think there should be a law that every board of trustees must hire somebody to see about the home conditions of the children, that they receive proper food etc I think we are coming to that We proposed it before, but we were turned down We are working on it now, and I think we will find a solution I believe the time will come when we will have an intelligent trained nurse to work for the interests of the children in every community in Indiana If we cannot keep our children well and strong in mind and body, they are not going to be effective citizens in years to come The school nurse, the school doctor, the school dentist are all part of the campaign for better things

We must secure more and better teachers improve on the quality of teachers that we have, and give them more money We were 38 000 teachers short in this country this past fall, and we have 65 000 below standard We are going to have to meet this situation by putting more money in the teacher's pay envelope You see there are practically 100 000 teaching positions in this country vacant or filled by folks who ought not to have them It does seem too bad to have to turn our children over to young, inexperienced girls in the schools, and there is only one way to get enough teachers, and that is to give them enough money

We simply must raise enough money thru taxes in this state to pay our teachers enough to live on We haven't been able to do it this year, so we will have to go thru the year short of teachers You say that a teacher should have the spirit of a missionary and not work merely for the money in it That is true, and they do, but they simply must have enough to live comfortably, and that is all they ask

What is the bank or the store or the farm compared to the child? I have often told the story of a man who was converted on that point He had an only son who lost his life during his college days The man said he would have willingly given all he had for the life of that boy

We parents must ask ourselves this question—it is a good way to make an estimate of the whole situation—What will our children think of us after we are dead and gone? If you can frame in your mind what it takes to make up the right kind of an answer in the thought of your children thirty or forty years from now you will see clearly where your duty lies

We haven't enough children in this country But if we will pay attention to the children we have, help them get the sort of education they ought to have, the sort of physical training they ought to have, we will work at the biggest job ever given men and women to do in this world That is what God thought when he established parenthood and put into our hands the care of these little children

And, in conclusion, my friends, I want to urge this matter of better schoolhouses, better health more teachers, more thoro equipment in the schools We must have them if we are to bring up our children to a strong and vigorous manhood and womanhood, and that is why we are holding this meeting today.

PHYSICAL EDUCATION IN THE PUBLIC SCHOOLS

GEORGE E SCHLAFER Supervisor of Courses in Play and Recreation, Extension Division, Indiana University

I have the advantage of most speakers because my subject admits of an unusual treatment If I see my audience getting sleepy I can put them thru a game or two by way of demonstration and waken them thoroly, still keeping within the province of my subject

According to Ritter, all living things that come to the earth are partly equipped for life the lower forms of life being more fortunate in this respect than the higher Insects are almost fully equipped The seventeen-year locusts spend a long period in preparing for a life of a very brief season Ascending in the scale of life, we find the higher forms less and less prepared until we reach man, the highest form, who requires years of preparation for life after he is born on the earth

Man is born with certain instincts which form the basis of his equipment for life, and it is upon and around these instincts that his preparation for life must be laid   One of these instincts is the play instinct   All forms of life desire a certain amount of physical activity, the higher forms requiring more than the lower   This physical activity means heat for the body   development of the lungs to furnish oxygen to the cells, and a good circulation of the blood to carry food to the tissues—processes necessary to the body at all times, but especially necessary during the period of growth   In order to have our boys and girls pass safely thru the stage of physical growth we must give back to childhood its heritage of active play   The growth of children into fully developed men and women is as natural as the growth of flowers or trees or birds unless the opportunities for growth are denied

It is objected that if play were instinctive, children would play under any conditions, and that there would be no need to teach them to play   But those who so object forget that we have interfered with children's opportunities to play by all sorts of artificial devices   We shut the children up in school, requiring them to keep quiet for long periods of time, doing our best to take all the "wiggle" out of them   Even the most staid grownups feel this desire to play   We see the august members of the state legislature breaking over all restraints, throwing books and papers about laughing and shouting across the room   and otherwise indulging their sense of play.

The play instinct differs somewhat from other instincts   It needs not only opportunity, as the instinct of walking or of talking, but needs also training   That form of education is good which is directed toward training natural instincts, not which seeks to crush or destroy them   The play instinct should be guided and directed, not repressed   For example, the instinct of combat, of contest, is a natural instinct   Two gangs of boys live in a neighborhood one on one side of the river, the other on the other side   Every day these boys meet and engage in quarrels and fights which must be settled   Can this instinct be crushed or can it be trained?   Organize these same gangs into two baseball teams, direct their play and watch the result   Play becomes a device to regulate and direct this instinct into proper channels, thereby using it to serve a social good, not destroying it or forcing it to express itself in undesirable ways

Many of the most important activities of our modern civilization are based on fundamental instincts—the hunting instinct, the fighting instinct which is expressed in many other ways than by the use of the fists, the exploring instinct, the building instinct turned to a hundred uses in our modern civilization, the cooperating instinct   the nurturing instinct whose expression is one of the most useful ones to the social order

Once in a while we meet the successful man who is a chronic objector to play   He urges as his excuse that he had no such 'foolishness' when he was a boy, therefore it is not essential to the life of any boy   But an inquiry into his case brings out the fact that his early life was spent on the farm where his many chores and duties satisfied his fundamental instincts, furnishing an outlet for his spirit of play and that as a matter of fact he did play

For the direction of the play instinct there should be special training, not necessarily special teachers but teachers with special training The ordinary teacher of spelling, of arithmetic, of reading, of geography, can be given special training to teach physical education and play In this connection we meet the objection that the teacher is already loaded down with extra work—that she is hired to teach the children to study, not to play, and that she has not time for both The difficulty with this argument is that study and play are too distinctly separated from each other in the popular mind, while as a matter of fact there is nothing paradoxical in their mixture Most persons think of the schoolroom as a place to study alone and make it a dull and dreary place indeed, where boys and girls are driven and not attracted to study.

I went to a school where the children had never played in the schoolroom, where they never laughed and never shouted in the building The teacher had grown gray in the service—she had reached that stage of maturity where she no longer cared for the play activity When I suggested that we play with the children in the schoolroom she was horrified at the idea of such a use for this place of study, and when I engaged the children in some good rousing games with lots of noise the teacher stood off in one corner with her hands over her ears But gradually as the play continued she joined in the fun, she caught her own spirit of youth That teacher will be good for another fifty years of service

Play of teacher with children means much for discipline, much for fellowship of teacher and child

Some games have advantages over others because of certain principles involved Those games should be played which, in the first place, emphasize exercise because they develop physical fitness We find boys and girls less physically fit during the school months Diseases most successfully attack them during the school year because of their lowered resistance

The draft boards of the war showed that we are not a healthy people. a little over one-fourth of our conscripted men were rejected because of defects of vital organs Our hearts, lungs arteries, and kidneys wear out We do not have strong, hard muscles We fall easy prey to pneumonia or typhoid fever

In the first place, games should be selected that make for good muscle development, for good vital organs that exercise the heart and lungs The infant is born with good vital organs, and care should be taken that his play and exercise keep these in good condition.

Second those games should be selected which require mental alertness The most active boy may be the dullest but games requiring mental alertness train mental ability.

Third, those games should be selected which train habits of character, those which develop a spirit of cooperation, of democracy, of self-control, of will power Anything which develops these qualities reflexively is acting in the right direction

In Iowa there is a wonderful bridge, the highest double span bridge in the world Before it was built it was said that such a structure was impossible Engineer after engineer worked on the problem and each in turn refused to undertake the task   Finally an engineer was found who agreed to build the bridge   When the great work was complete many came to view it and to congratulate the engineer on the structure   But he said . "That which you see is not my work, that is the work of my men   I will show you my work '   And he took them down to a depth of forty feet below the bed of the river and, pointing to the foundation stones, he said, "That is my building "

Training in physical education and play is building on the instincts, on the genuine foundation stones of human life

SAFETY FIRST

H E MEGINNES, Safety Agent for the Pennsylvania Railroad

"Safety First" may seem rather a strange subject for an address before an assembly like this but I believe I can explain before I get thru that you women can do a wonderful lot in helping in this great work   At the present time, no doubt you all know the federal controlled railroads of the United States are 178 in number, and they are having a National Accident Prevention Drive   To date, we have reduced personal injuries among the employees of the railroad about 75 or 80 per cent

At the present time, we scarcely pick up a newspaper that we do not read of some horrible accident at a railroad crossing, where an automobile has been struck and one or more people seriously injured or killed   There seems to be too much dependence put on the human element, in other words, the crossing watchman, and they don't observe the sign which appears at almost every railroad crossing, "Stop Look, and Listen"   I heard a man say the other day that if we all practiced carefulness we would never have any regrets   Our statistics show that 95 per cent of all personal injuries that occur to the employees of the Pennsylvania Railroad are due to carelessness, and I believe that percentage would be true among the general public

Every year we have 5,000 trespassers killed on the railroad   Now, by trespassers we don't mean tramps   We mean citizens, and a great proportion of those 5,000 are children   These trespassers get in the habit of using the railroad tracks as a highway, and walk thru the railroad yards, and, as the old story that we have all heard so many times tells of the pitcher that goes to the well once too often, they are injured

Last fall, in the northern part of the state, one of our township school wagons was struck on a railroad crossing and six children were killed and six badly injured   I believe you know that there is a law on the statute books of the state of Indiana that all drivers of township wagons must stop and have a responsible occupant of the wagon go forward cross the track and look both ways before they signal the driver to come ahead I believe it was not done in this case, and we all know the results   Last week a school wagon was struck near Toledo, Ohio, and two occupants were killed

You women can help in this work by having your children, if they go to school in the township wagons, tell you of any infraction of this law by the driver of the wagon, and you in turn can take it up with the trustee in your township. That will no doubt be the means of compelling the drivers to observe the law. They will soon find out that they will be reported if they do not observe the law, and they will no doubt be more careful than they have been in the past.

A few weeks ago I was in the northern part of the state, standing on a station platform and noticed a school wagon drive across the track without stopping. I was able to find out from some people who were standing on the platform the name of the driver, and wrote to the township trustee of that township and asked him to call the attention of the driver to this infraction of the law. Recently we addressed letters to the township trustees in all the townships thru which the Pennsylvania Railroad operates in the state of Indiana, asking them if they wouldn't cooperate with us and see that the drivers obeyed the law governing drivers of school wagons.

If each and every one of us becomes interested in this work, we will be able to save a great many lives and limbs, and I don't know of anything that is more noble than this work. In closing, I want to appeal to all of you to do everything you can to help in this work. If you are in the habit of driving an automobile yourself, or riding with anyone else, don't permit them to cross a railroad without stopping. The driver lots of times doesn't realize how near the train is. It may not be in sight, it may be coming around a curve, and maybe he doesn't hear the whistle or the ringing of the bell. Sometimes the fraction of a second will mean death and disaster.

A locomotive engineer on one of the southwestern railroad kept a record for thirty days of the near-accidents he had with his train, and in that period of time he came within a few feet of striking sixteen automobiles. What must the figures be for near-accidents for all the railroad engineers, and how many unfortunates were there in the United States who did not escape but who were either killed or badly injured!

THE STATE—AN OFFENDER

JAMES A. COLLINS, Judge of Marion County Criminal Court

Child welfare is, I take it, the underlying thought of this convention. Within the scope of that subject are all of the problems of humanity. Ignorance, intemperance and poverty, those missionaries of crime, are ever at work recruiting the great army of delinquents and leaving in their wake every problem affecting child welfare.

All-absorbing as the great problems of industrial strife and social unrest are, and overshadowing as they do almost every other concern in life, yet we cannot lose sight of the fact that we still have and will continue to have our problems of dependency and delinquency. Insane and feeble-minded deaf and dumb, blind and infirm, felon and misdemeanant, the wards of every commonwealth, will continue to present problems the solution of which will demand the best thought and attention of our citizenship.

It is with pardonable pride that I say it,—Indiana is excelled by no other state in the Union in the treatment of her dependent and delinquent wards. Splendid as her record is, great as her achievements are, there still remain unsolved many problems the product of our complex citizenship.

So interrelated are all of the social problems of the state that it occurred to me that a discussion of a phase rarely touched upon would not be out of place on this occasion   Thruout the one hundred years of our existence as a commonwealth we have failed and neglected to give adequate consideration to the children of those committed to our penal institutions   This neglect has been brutal and has made the state an offender   This offending has arisen from a failure to enact needed legislation and to repeal odious and obsolete laws

The children of the convict, like all others born under the Stars and Stripes, are potential citizens and as such are entitled to the same opportunity for education and development as is accorded all other children   It is true that this intervening circumstance arising in the life of a child may force it to become a ward of the state and its development into full free citizenship retarded or destroyed

Our failure to interpret the spirit of the Constitution and enact the legislation it enjoins is responsible for this offending   The Constitution of Indiana contains the sublime injunction that ' The penal code shall be founded upon the principles of reformation and not vindictive justice."   For eighty-one years the annunciation of that great humane principle remained a mere collection of words   But in 1897 the legislature made its first attempt to apply this principle to the administration of justice by enacting the indeterminate sentence law, which provided a minimum and maximum prison term   Under its provisions the trustees of the penal institutions were given the power to parole prisoners at the expiration of the minimum term   By abolishing the old system of measuring out a definite amount of punishment for so much crime, the state speaking thru this statute, said to those coming within its provisions "The restoration of your liberty is largely within your own hands "   The enactment of the Juvenile Court law in 1903 and the suspended sentence law in 1907 were both applications of this great principle   The passage of the law providing for the State Farm for petty offenders came more nearly embodying the true spirit of the Constitution than any former legislation   In thus providing a proper place other than the county jail for the confinement of misdemeanants it was the first real movement in the solution of the crime problem.

These laws, enacted since 1897, are the milestones marking the progress of humane legislation   Splendid and beneficent as they are, they do not completely fulfil the mandate of the Constitution   It was never intended under so sublime and exalted an injunction to confiscate the labor of the man behind the wall!   It was never intended to provide for the infamous system known as "contract labor" in our penal institutions'   It was never intended to increase poverty and misery by completely depriving the wife and children of their only hope for support'   It was never intended to permit corporations or individuals to wax rich on the labor of the state's delinquent, and at the expiration of his term of imprisonment, to place in his hands the princely sum of $5 and a railroad ticket back to his family '   No, the framers of our Constitution had a broader vision'   They could see the wage-earner entering prison deprived of his liberty but with bodily health and vigor, capable of earning something for his dependents, and so they said, "reformation and not vindictive justice"

To the everlasting credit of Governor James P Goodrich, contract labor in penal institutions has been abolished   This legislation, enacted by the

General Assembly of 1917, will not become effective until 1920 It fails, however to make any provision for the compensation of the inmates

Why we have never made provision for the remuneration of the inmates of our penal institutions is difficult to understand Every governor and legislator every judge and prosecuting attorney every warden and superintendent has known of the misery and poverty flowing to dependents thru our present prison system "How am I going to support myself and children if you send my husband to the penitentiary?' is the pitiful interrogatory that has been propounded to every judicial officer in every state in the Union They could only answer it by directing the poverty-stricken wife to the nearest charity. I recently committed a young man to the Reformatory He was guilty of a series of crimes and I had no alternative. After his sentence I saw a little woman leave the courtroom crying bitterly I later learned that on the following day she became a mother She must rear her little one in absolute poverty during the father's incarceration because the state has failed to make any provision for their support I presented this matter to Governor Goodrich and, while he was in hearty sympathy with any plan for the amelioration of such conditions, he said. "The difficulty is securing legislation that would solve this problem"

With the approval of the governor, a bill was presented to the last session of the legislature providing for the appointment of a commission to investigate and report to the next General Assembly on a plan for the compensation of inmates of penal institutions This bill passed the House with but two dissenting votes On reaching the Senate it was referred to a committee whose chairman promptly recommended that the bill be indefinitely postponed for the reason, as he said "there were altogether too many commissions" This action was taken before an opportunity was given to present the merits of the bill Common courtesy it seems to me should have delayed any action until even a "wise" senator could be informed of the purposes of the proposed legislation

Permit me to say now that at the next session of the General Assembly a bill will be presented providing for a compensation plan for the inmates of penal institutions and its sponsors will be the best citizenship of this state

No compensation plan would be equitable that did not contemplate all of the inmates of an institution In our own institutions and in those of many other states, where inmates earn sums for labor performed in excess of the task, no provision is made for the compensation of those inmates in charge of the kitchen dining-room, and hospital Yet without this service the earning power of the inmate would be nil

Compensation for inmates of penal institutions is not a theory Such a plan has been in successful operation at Stillwater Minn and the inmates have received as high as $75 000 in wages in a single year A similar plan is in operation in Virginia. In speaking of the plan at Stillwater, Warden Reed said "I believe Minnesota has in a way as nearly solved the problem of prison labor as any state in the Union The money that these men earned was sent to their families if they had any If a man does not earn enough to provide for his family and the family is destitute, we have a state aid law that supplies the family No children are kept from school in our state by reason of the father or mother being in prison, neither are they in want. I believe that the salvation of the inmates in prison is profitable work. I don't believe it is right to expect men to work at their best if they are paid nothing. I believe our prisons should have such a degree of efficiency that they can afford to pay the men."

In the State Prison at Michigan City, Warden Fogarty has developed the binder-twine plant into a great industry, with an annual capacity of 6,000,000 pounds of twine. The labor is all performed by inmates and the earnings go to the state. Other industries in that institution are under contracts which will be abolished in 1920. Many of the inmates employed in these industries earn sums for labor performed in excess of their tasks.

At the Reformatory at Jeffersonville a large number of inmates are earning money at the industries established there. However, there is no definite plan that contemplates all the inmates.

The Indiana State Farm for misdemeanants is hardly old enough to make a showing but it has possibilities that should make it a self-supporting institution with an ample surplus to provide compensation for the inmates.

We in Indiana are not so far behind our sister states in working out the problem of inmate labor but the weakness in our system is the failure to provide for either the inmate or his family to enjoy a little of the fruit of his labor.

The effect of this present system has been a disastrous one to paroled men. With the meager amount allowed them by the state, they are unable to tide over the period required in obtaining employment and are soon returned to the institution as parole violators. This condition could be avoided and parole violations reduced to a minimum thru the medium of a compensation plan for inmates as above suggested.

With the annual cost of maintaining our penal and benevolent institutions reaching more than $3,000,000 annually, is it not time that we take counsel of the fathers and make our Constitution something more than a sounding brass and a tinkling cymbal? Shall we go on increasing the burden on the state or shall we by the enactment of just and humane legislation lighten the load now borne by the commonwealth?

I am not unmindful of the fact that there are influences responsible for some of this burden that cannot be effected by legislation. Upon the shoulders of judges and prosecuting attorneys must be placed some of the responsibility for our ever-increasing prison population. A few years ago I was at the State Prison and while there seated in the warden's office I heard the stories of ten prisoners. Nine out of the ten had no business there. From all the facts obtainable in the nine cases it was fair to assume that upon a trial and finding in Marion county none would have received a sentence in excess of six months on the State Farm. But in the counties where they were indicted in each instance they had been cajoled by a tyro filling the office of prosecuting attorney, into entering a plea of guilty to the felony and upon the plea were sentenced to the State Prison. Little relief can be obtained from this situation until we stop making the office of prosecuting attorney a prize for the graduating classes of our law schools. This important office should be sought by the best lawyer residing in a circuit. What inducement is there for a lawyer of ability to seek this office the income of which rests almost entirely upon fees? These fees are derived largely from the prosecution of misdemeanors, which represent a class of cases that are distasteful to decent members of the bar. While such a system might have been warranted in the pioneer days of this commonwealth there can be no argument advanced for its continuance. And what is true of the fee system as to prosecuting attorneys is likewise true of the same system as it relates to justices of the peace and constables. All forms of fees in connection with the administration of justice are wrong in theory and pernicious in practice, and are in contravention of the spirit of our Constitution. The laws permitting these evils to exist are odious and should be repealed. So long as they remain on the statute books, so long will the state be an offender.

The enactment of the law providing for a penal farm was intended primarily to do away with the vicious system of jail sentences which had converted our jails into prisons. This jail problem will remain with us so long as the state countenances that piece of petty political graft—paying sheriffs 40 cents a day for feeding prisoners. Every prisoner in a county jail is a state prisoner. The state should furnish him his food and not the sheriff. I am in favor of the sheriffs receiving a proper compensation for their services in caring for prisoners but I am unalterably opposed to the system that permits them to profit upon their misfortunes. So long as the state permits the jails to be used as prisons, so long will she be an offender.

The system under which a husband and father is incarcerated for his failure to pay a money fine smacks strongly of the old English system of imprisonment for debt. He is committed to the jail or the workhouse not because the court gave him a term of imprisonment, but because he is poor.

It was demonstrated during my term as city judge of Indianapolis that this legal antiquity could be successfully abolished. I introduced the plan for the collection of money fines on instalments, saving more than 3,500 persons the odium of imprisonment. These persons were released on probation to pay their fines under this plan. They paid into the court in four years $34,014 without a scratch of a pen for security. All on an honor basis! Such a plan could be put into operation in every court exercising criminal jurisdiction. To insure the successful working of such a plan throughout the state, the present law should be amended so as to give judges the power to parole persons for a definite period in which to pay their fines. The law under which money fines are now stand is obsolete and should be amended as suggested.

This plan for the payment of money fines by instalments is only social justice. Governor Goodrich is the first governor of the commonwealth to work out this plan in the cases of persons paroled from the jail or the state farm. The people generally do not understand that at the expiration of a term of imprisonment in the case of a misdemeanant that he must lay out the fine and costs at the rate of $1 a day if unable to pay the same. To prevent injustice and to return the wage-earner to his family was the basis for the establishment of this new method in dealing with delinquents. The plan simple as it is not only benefits the individual and his family but it protects the common school fund to which all money fines must go. Of all requests for parole that are recommended by the judge of the criminal court of Marion county, 75 per cent are based on this plan.

My friends, I trust that we at this conference may grasp the spirit of our basic law and have the courage to advocate the legislation necessary to right the wrongs and evils that have dwarfed its majestic and sublime principles

I trust we may go from this conference with a new vision of our relation toward God and man, emphasizing with the immortal Burns,

> The rank is but the guinea's stamp
> The man's the Gowd for a' that

MOTHERS OF MEN

Mrs. Alice French, American War Mothers, Indianapolis

I feel like quoting Mr. Hoke, "My subject is a whopper."

There was but one motherless man and that was Adam. He named the wife that was given to him Eve, because she was to be the mother of men. Why the name of Eve has been the synonym for all scheming, maneuvering women since, I do not know. We still have Adams who say "She tempted me."

During the last few years we have realized the seriousness of being the mothers of men. The pages of history will not record a greater battle fought and won than that of the war mothers in the last few years. As we rocked our sons in the cradle of dreams we pictured each one as a great citizen. We looked upon each as a possible president of the United States. As an indication of the persistence of this idea in our mother minds, look over the names of our sons on the conscription lists and see how many bore the names of presidents. As we reared our sons we tested our every act, our every step by their future happiness and good. We truly lived for them. And then when the war came on we found our life hopes blighted. We could understand how everybody else's son could go but ours. Our hearts stood still.

When the first call came, my son's name was not on the list, but there were so many exemptions in Marion county, because of defects, that 600 new names were drawn to fill the quota. My son's name was one of the first. I still had one hope. I thought he would not be accepted on account of a weak heart. He said he would go down to take the physical examination at ten. I was not greatly worried; I thought they would not take him. A little later he telephoned from downtown, "I got by, mother. I have been accepted." I asked, "Did you ask for exemption?" and he replied "No, why should I?"

I put my hands over my eyes. I had built high hopes for his future, I had given him the best education money could buy. Now the books were to be closed, the door was to be locked, his career was to be ended. When he put on his uniform, and passed out the gate, and waved me goodbye, I felt that the end of everything had come

As the months went by we mothers who had had this common experience began to be some consolation to each other. Gradually the heartaches began to be replaced by pride, as we told the wonderful qualities of our sons. We mothers thought we would write a history of our boys, but we found that each boy would require several volumes, so we decided to wait a few years, thinking that by that time we might be able to include two or three boys in the same book.

As I look over a company of war mothers I feel that I am looking upon the finest specimens of American womanhood. These mothers have a common tie, because of a great common experience. They are women of mature judgment. The mother's love has been likened to the love of God. National problems would be safe if they could be handled and settled by war mothers. At Washington how quickly the war mothers decided questions by a large majority! The right is always popular and public opinion easily decides the right.

In our organization only mothers of the flesh are eligible. We have this ruling because we feel that otherwise complications will arise. We expect to be of the same size as the American Legion. When the boys first came home I asked my son "What are you going to call your organization?" and he said, "Sons of the War Mothers."

The mother influence is a powerful one thruout life. I believe everyone remembers some principle or some trait of his mother that will cling to him thru life. The memory of my mother is one of roses and quiet Sabbaths. Yesterday a gentleman said to me, "We have no Sabbath any more." I do not believe it is quite so bad as that, but I do think we are getting away from it. I believe this lack of quietness, this lack of a day of rest is one of the causes of the present social unrest. We need the Sabbath as a day of physical rest, we need it for spiritual reflection. Its observance is based on scientific findings. It was given to us as a day for our use. I clearly recall the quiet Sabbath that my mother had in our home and I must say that the things we do today on the Sabbath grate on my feelings and make me anxious about our future.

I am much concerned over the teaching of social hygiene in the schools. I am glad to see that the Parent-Teacher Association decided that this is a problem for the home. I think it certainly is. Those who advocate its teaching in the schools will but defeat their own ends. It is a thing which we mothers should have exclusively to ourselves. One of the most beautiful experiences I have ever had in my home was to sit down with my son and talk things over. He had a delightful way of whispering about things as tho they were confidential—just for the two of us. The mother can train her children in the home in a way that is not possible in the school. And I am quite sure that the teachers do not want this added burden.

There is a great difference between the sons who went away from us to war and the sons who came back to us. This difference is that they came back men. They decide quickly and directly. If they can only communicate this quality to older men we may be able to eliminate some of the contention and struggle and strife of the present day. As in the garden of Eden we have in this America of ours everything we ought to want and yet we are struggling for the things that we haven't whether we need them or not.

For the mothers whose boys went West we have the greatest tenderness and sympathy. It meant the setting of a great hope when these boys went West with the setting of the sun. We look up to God's Service Flag and see the gold star twinkling there for a mother's consolation. There is a

halo about these mother faces and a gentle resignation that can come only
from God himself

Now that the boys are home we are proud of them and proud to be
ourselves that these our sons are men and we the mothers of men

THE REAL MEETING-PLACE OF THE HOME AND SCHOOL

REV FRANK S C WICKS, All Souls' Unitarian Church, Indianapolis

In discussing this subject today I hope I appear as modest as I feel
I do not stand triumphant at the end of the road the problem solved and
tell you how you, too, may arrive Mine is not the satisfaction of solving
the problem but the zest of pursuing it I share the chase with you, and
together we may drive it into a corner where it may be slain We know
what Margaret Fuller felt when she cried "I am the parent of an infinite
soul God be merciful to me, a sinner' The teachers who share the
problem with us may echo "I am the teacher of an infinite soul" And in
chorus we cry, 'Who is sufficient for these things?"

The question before us is what is the real meeting-place of the home
and the school The answer is the child There our interests meet, our
duties begin our attention comes to a focus Our common interest is in
the growing soul We want that soul to develop into that perfect symme-
try for which nature designed it

The child is not a thing to be hacked and hewed and beaten into some
form which will enable it to fit into a mechanical society It is an organ-
ism with its own laws of growth

Each human being is an end in himself and not merely an instrument
to be used for purposes beyond himself This was the viciousness of the
Prussian system of education no child was considered as an end in himself
He was so much plastic building material to be used in the construction of
a powerful and all-absorbing state The question becomes not only one of
the real meeting-place of the home and school, but the meeting-place of the
school and state We may have a splendid system for the making of a
machine, but one utterly destructive of human souls

We perceive a gap between the home and school thru which children
drop into an abyss of ignorance—ignorance of the worst kind—ignorance
of half-knowledge We want to know how this gap may be filled and how
a straight path may be made between the home and the school Our aim is
all right It is to achieve harmony thru cooperation Both parents and
teachers want the same thing They are asking how to bring about this
achievement of harmony This as I see it is the one object of the Parent
Teacher Association

We recognize where we have failed We parents are willing to begin
by blaming ourselves Teachers may make their own confessions We
have sent our children to school with a sigh of relief We have shifted our
responsibility to the school We have thought of the school as a machine
where the raw material goes in at one end and comes out at the other a
finished product

The Mother is now following the Child into the school and asking "How
can I help?" But the American Father! I wish I had him here He is
the kind of father we once conceived God to be a stern judge, keeping

severe account of the misdeeds of his children, meting out deserved punishment. Christians have placed a pitying son beside him to temper his justice with mercy, and Catholics have put a mother there as well. Even the divine government needs to be that of a family. Spencer says that if the fathers of England would devote as much time and interest in raising their children as they do in improving the breed of their hogs we should soon have a superior race.

My father was a typical American father. He never visited the school. He knew the teacher's name only as he saw it signed at the bottom of a note saying that Frank had been a naughty boy. Being a resourceful lad, I could always convince him that I had been a victim of injustice, and so escaped parental chastisement. He did not think much of that teacher.

Think of parents entrusting a child to a teacher and not knowing the teacher or what the teacher is doing with their child! We may assume that the teacher is intellectually fitted for her vocation. But is she physically fitted? Temperamentally fitted?

If she is lacking at any point how may we help her in overcoming the deficiency? We must become acquainted with the teacher and permit her to become acquainted with us, that she in turn may know where our deficiencies are. How about her physical fitness? It takes health and strength to teach successfully. The teacher who appears in the schoolroom in the morning pale, tired, nervous, irritable, is so because of some cause. We have no right to put her to the inquisition. But we can establish friendly relationship with her and then with tact and sympathy learn the cause of her physical unfitness.

Do the conditions of her life make for health? Has she the right kind of a hygienic environment? Is she in a home where she can find rest and peace in her leisure time? Or is she precipitated into the many cares and drudgeries of the home? Is there an invalid mother or father? or a sister to whom she must give the last ounce of her strength? Can she sleep in the fresh air? Does she have proper food? What kind of transportation does she have? Does she arrive at the school tired out after an hour's ride in a street car hanging onto a strap? I know of such a typical case in which the teacher lives in the extreme northwest part of the city and teaches in a school in the extreme northeast. In such a case could you suggest that she be transferred to a school nearer home, or if she can move conveniently find her a good boarding-place near her school?

How about her luncheon? How is she compelled to spend her evenings? In correcting papers? Then buy her a waste basket. How should her evenings be spent? Certainly in the way most agreeable to her.

Is she able to enjoy the best things in music, art, literature, the drama? How many of you saw to it that your teacher had opportunity to hear the grand opera last Monday night? Do you know that several cultured teachers could not go because this theater does not admit those whose color is a little too dark?

Much of this is a financial problem.

It goes without saying that the home and school are the meeting-places for parents and teachers. Have you given the teacher an opportunity to know you in your home? It is just as important for the teacher to know you in your home as for you to know the teacher in the classroom. The teacher needs to know the background of the child   The child from the cultured home needs different instruction from that of the child whose home lacks cultural influence

Does the child hear good English in the home?   If the English language is maltreated in the home it is almost impossible to teach it in the school After all these years of public schools we wonder at the longevity of the 'ain't" and   ham't" and the persistence of double negatives   Just now in my own house we are trying to eradicate a superfluity of negatives from the vocabulary of a child   "I haven t got none   is the state of her present plight   She came from a home where good English was not spoken and if she had continued in that home the school would have labored in vain

Have you ever watched children play school at home?   What is most prominent in their playing teacher?   Too often as I have watched them it is chiefly reprimands, punishments cross looks severe tones   Where did they learn those?

To balance the case the teacher has a pretty good knowledge of us thru our children   She knows whether or not we enforce obedience.   She knows whether we have taught the child that crying, coaxing, whining, or anger gets what he wants

So parents blame teachers and teachers blame parents and from blame no good can come   When home and school have found their meeting-place parents and teachers can talk over in a friendly way problems which the other method fails to solve

Of necessity the attitude of parents is intensely individual   Their child is unique   Of necessity the attitude of the teacher is predominantly impersonal   The child who is one of forty must be treated as one of a group In this meeting of parents and teachers the parent will become more impersonal and the teacher more personal in their respective attitudes

I could suggest a hundred problems at that common meeting-place and each will help in the solution   These problems of education are the biggest problems in the world and the most worth while   When our present problems are solved new ones will arise   We must not be discouraged   This growing human nature which we are trying to train into erect fine manhood is good stuff, the best in the world   It is the stuff out of which God-like men and women are made   If we worked alone, if the stuff itself were refractory, we might despair   But we do not work alone   There is a Power that worketh with us, a Power constantly at work lifting us to the height where we are but little lower than the angels

VOCATIONAL GUIDANCE

G I CHRISTIE, Superintendent of the Department of Agricultural
Extension Purdue University

One goes to school not so much to gain knowledge as to gain power not so much to learn to know things as to learn to do things "—President Lawrence

If we can keep those lines before us and perhaps align our future work a little more nearly to them, then I will have accomplished any purpose that may have been in the minds of those who invited me to talk

How many schools are working along that line at this time? I happen to be a member of a Parent-Teacher Club and have one child in school It is of some interest to me, during the few hours that I am at home and get a chance to talk with my daughter, to find out just how nearly the instruction that she is receiving is in line with these words I have just given you

In the grade in which she is now enrolled, she is supposed to have some agriculture, and she tells me something of what she receives A few days ago she said to me, "Father, there isn't any interest shown by our class in agriculture The girls just hate it" And I said, "What is the matter? Doesn't the teacher show you samples of soils and doesn't he carry on demonstrations, and doesn't he show you how the water runs down thru the soil, and then, by capillary attraction, goes up thru the soil, and doesn't he tell you about how organic matter works in it, and a lot of other things?" She said, "No, we haven't had anything like that" "How are you going to get any agriculture if you don't see these things so that you will get them in your mind?' I asked She replied, "Father, don't you understand, we are not supposed to see anything but the teacher and the book?"

And so, in her first few lessons in the class it was quite clearly impressed upon her mind that she was supposed to keep her eyes and her mind on the teacher and the book That is a fault that is found in the majority of the lessons that are taught in the schools over our state Teachers are holding the children to the book, and these children are getting their lessons and they are reciting and writing compositions and getting high grades and passing from one section and division to the other. After they are graduated from our institutions and you ask them what they can do, they simply reply. We never thought of that

When boys come out of our high schools, we are told that they are unable even to fill out a check they are unable to recognize a note in the bank, they are unable to compute measurements They are unable to work in the stores without much training They are unable to work with any kind of tools or implements They are unable to explain any better than before they went to school what they have in the garden or what they have on the farm or what they deal with in the home And so we wonder. when we see this condition, if the instruction in the school is related to the home or the farm or the shop or the store or the bank or whether the work in the school is something that has been designed and calculated on the part of instructors themselves simply to lead children from one stage in mathematics to another, and from one line in English to another without any reference to the things that they are going to have to do in the days that are to come

This condition has brought much criticism on the schools, but, worst of all, it has driven boys and girls out of the schoolroom, has separated them from education and therefore has placed on the farms and in the homes and in industry everywhere thousands upon thousands of boys and girls who are classed as illiterate, who are separated from the ideals of a democracy, who are failing to get the grasp of a greater Americanism, and who are failing to do the things that help to build up either individual or community or state or country

You know, when the boys were drafted into camp, they were given certain tests, and one test was to find out how much they knew from what they had learned in school. They based this test on about the fourth grade. They were required to write their names, to add a few figures and do simple multiplication. The boys who came out of these wonderful schools of which we speak, and out of this great system of public education supported by taxes, supported by state and federal governments —when these boys, the best in the land, were called upon to write their own names and to add two and two together and say that it meant four, 23 per cent were classed as illiterate.

Now, friends, if we have schools in this day and age, 1919, that are taking the boys of the homes of Indiana, holding them for two and three years, and filling them with hatred and disgust for education and are turning them away without interest in education, then surely there is a call for some sort of change in the kind of work that is being carried on.

We like to say a lot of the good things about our schools, but I believe we have come to a time when we might just as well be honest with ourselves and honest with those about us and seek for the troubles that do exist in these institutions, and then let us set about to correct them.

We are talking today about this great subject of vocational guidance. It is a fine subject to put on the program, but I want to say to you frankly that I haven't found anybody yet that knows very much about it. They know vocational guidance is a nice term, but the definition of vocational guidance is something that hasn't been given to us in an understandable way, and just how to carry out vocational guidance is something that I would hesitate to outline or describe to you this afternoon because I don't think I know, and I don't know anybody else that does know. But the happy part of it is that there are a large number of people working at it, and when we get people to thinking, and when we get them to striving and to organizing and to demonstrating and to working, it is only going to be a short time until we will find out a great deal more than we know now about how to determine the vocational needs of boys and girls and how to direct them in the big things that they ought to do.

You know the story of the teacher who had gone into a new school. Everything was brand new. It was spick and span. The ideal was to maintain it in that condition for a long time, and so they were deeply interested. About the second day the teacher walked down the aisle and he found there a fellow just closing up a jack-knife, after having carved his name or his initials in the top of his desk. Now, the first inclination of that teacher was just to reach down and grab that boy by the back of the neck and lift him out of the seat and give him a shaking and some pretty severe punishment. Then he said to himself, "I don't believe that will do." And so he went away and he thought about it. He went back again and gazed on the initials as they were carved in the desk, and he found that the boy had done a most beautiful job, and about as nearly perfect in the way of carving initials as he had ever seen. He said to himself "Since this boy shows an aptitude for carving, perhaps we had better give him some work along that line." So he made arrangements for him to go down into the manual training department, and he was given special instruction. Today, that boy ranks as one of our great architects. It would have been easy for that teacher by severe discipline by interfering with the boy at that time simply to have wrecked the whole future of his life. But thru a perception of what that boy was capable of doing, he directed him along lines in which he has developed as one of the large and strong and influential men of this country.

So you know a great many stories of boys and girls whose aptitude for certain lines of work has been determined. Now, if it were possible to take every boy and girl and sit down with them and study them and study their work and determine just exactly what they could do best, that would be my ideal of vocational guidance.

But friends, with the thousands and hundreds of thousands and millions of boys and girls thruout the land in the schools, and the impossibility of reaching them in an individual way, it is an entirely impossible task at the present time. We have to approach it in a different way.

Let us see some of the things we do to avoid getting at any vocational guidance or any vocational direction. We feel we have one of the best school systems to be found anywhere in the country. We are very glad to have our friends who come to Indianapolis at this time tell us of the wonderful educational system in Indiana, and we believe it and are proud of it, and we are pleased to hear them say it. Yet there is one feature of the school system of Indiana that is absolutely wrong, and until it is corrected we are going to undo thru that medium a large amount of the good that we are attempting thru the school year.

We open our schools usually in early September and we place in these schools the best men and women that can be hired, men and women with training and instruction, men and women accustomed to handling children, men and women who know how to guide them and direct them. These teachers are given charge of the boys and girls from early September on thru until the first of next June. Then, when the sun's rays become a little hot and the days become long and the teacher becomes tired, we say "Well, vacation time is here and we will close up this school because the teacher wants a vacation, or the teacher wants to go to summer school, or the children ought to have a rest." Then we proceed to close the schools at once all over this state. The children are turned out into the streets, and there they are for three months. In Terre Haute and Fort Wayne and Indianapolis and Evansville and all the other cities of the state, the streets are filled with boys and girls without any direction or guidance of these teachers of whom we have just been speaking. We know there are a few parents who are able to take their boys and girls and carry them off to the lakes or to some resort, and there they will have healthful sport and they will grow strong and prepare themselves for the trials and tribulations of another school year. But the majority of the boys and girls cannot go away. They are there in the city and so they go down to "the old swimmin' hole" and out to the old baseball diamond. They sit around on the street, and they get into back yards behind the barn, or they gather in groups here and there and everywhere, and by one means and another they undo in a few months in the summer-time a large share of the good that has been accomplished during the school year. It is because of the troubles, it is because of the mischief, it is because of the bad habits that are developed during vacations that we fill the institutions out here at

Plainfield and Clermont and the other institutions of the state, because these children thruout the summer months are without any guidance except what the busy fathers and mothers can give them

If we want to do something in Indiana for vocational guidance, there is one wonderful opportunity No boy or girl should be turned out of the Indiana schools and called upon to go his or her way without something definite to do Now, it may be a garden It may be raising some chickens It may be keeping a pig It may be raising some corn It may be working in a factory It may be driving a delivery wagon It may be working in the house It may be knitting or sewing or store work But boys and girls should have something to do in the open air that is going to allow them to develop and grow strong and utilize the mind as well as the hand Otherwise, with these long, idle weeks and months, we know we are going to undo much of the good that the teachers have attempted to do during the school year

In one of our counties they have decided this year that they wanted the children to do definite things Heretofore in the rural communities, the objection to having boys and girls do things has been that it was always done for father or for mother The boy was given a calf to raise, and when the calf grew up father claimed it for his cow and he sold it The boy was given a colt He fed the colt and took care of it, but when it grew up, it was father's horse. When he took a pig and grew it, father sold it with his lot That is the criticism that has been upon our homes and our parents, because they didn't allow the boys and girls to have some proprietary interest in the work that they did Down in Sullivan county, they have decided this year that they are going to give 500 boys and girls a trip this coming spring at the close of the school They said to those boys and girls "You will get that trip if you do a definite piece of work this winter and then that work earn enough money to make the trip If you raise a pig, it is understood when you start the pig is yours and when it is sold the money is supposed to be used to pay for that trip If you keep the chickens, take care of the hens or do certain chores, you are to be paid for it and then the money is to be used in making this trip" The parents have agreed to the plan Five hundred boys and girls are now enrolled and in all cases have practically raised their $20 which will be required to make the trip

There is an example of some guidance, because fathers and mothers and trustees and everybody in the community are interested in that very thing, and they are interested from the day it was announced and on thru all these long winter months The boys and girls have something to work for, they have something to think about They are doing their task in the best known way because they want some money out of it, and they have to do it right or they won't get credit for it in their schools Then when they do the work and the money comes it is going to be theirs, and they are going to take that money and spend it for themselves and they are going to make that trip and have a good time

Over in one of our cities just a little east of Tippecanoe county there is a school where they have never been able to interest the boys and girls in a satisfactory way They have put in a vocational teacher there recently He has had them thru the teachers of his school, writing lessons on history, he has had them writing stories on English Then one of his boys, he told us yesterday, couldn t get what he wanted to write upon so he said to him "If you will go to the Presbyterian Church Sunday morning and listen to the sermon and then come back and write that up, I will give you credit on the story that you write" This boy not only went to church and heard the sermon, but came home and wrote the story and it was so good that it was published in the paper of Elwood night before last This is guidance, because you have the boy doing something that connects him up with real life, connects him up with the church in this case—brings him in contact with the newspaper in the town, and it has made him believe and understand that he is somebody and that he is capable of doing something if he will go about it in the right way

We know then, that these pupils should be given some work thruout their school terms that will interest them These boys and girls who have gone out of school and have not been interested in the work should be brought back Thru the vocational courses supported by the vocational law in Indiana and the federal law known as the Smith-Hughes law, it is possible now with the aid of the vocational teachers, to go out and interest boys and girls and bring them back in the school, and establish projects where the work is carried on right on the boy's own farm, or right in the girl's own home, and carried on in such a way that they are getting definite results

I know of one school not very far away where they took up home economics They put in this work against much opposition They put it in tho the people didn't see the value of it It was a school down in an industrial section where patrons were all hard-working people The first demonstration that the teacher gave the girls in home economics was in the cooking of creamed asparagus on toast Now, when those children went home and told their parents of the kind of instruction they were going to get in home economics, there was no asparagus on toast there, and those people were not going to buy asparagus, and they knew by a hard day's work that they had put in from early morning until late at night in that manufacturing plant that it was going to take just a little more than creamed asparagus on toast to sustain father and brother So there wasn't very much interest shown in the home economics work Criticism was made of the course and the people called upon the teacher to change her ways The result is that the course has been entirely changed, and it is now down on a practical basis

One of the teachers, in connection with a campaign on milk in Evansville, selected a large number of boys and girls, and then found out thru one means and another what those boys and girls were eating This teacher found that those boys and girls were getting coffee and fried potatoes and fried pork and bread for breakfast, and then they were getting bread without any butter fried potatoes and fried pork and coffee for dinner, and then they were getting fried pork and fried potatoes and black coffee and bread without butter for supper These boys and girls were supposed to go to school and spend their hours there and study their lessons and get along But the teacher found that they weren't enthusiastic, they didn't have any inspiration In the slang of the school, they didn't have the "pep   The teacher suggested a change in the menu   She substituted for fried pork and fried potatoes cream of wheat with good cream, and she substituted for coffee glasses of rich milk, with the result that in the ten days that the test was carried on the girls and boys not only increased in weight, but they showed increased interest in their school work   Their color improved and the health and the wholesomeness and the spirit of the whole room was changed simply because they found out what food was needed

As a result of this little demonstration which was put on in the schools and a campaign which followed thru the Rotary, Kiwanis, and other clubs of Evansville, it was found that the week following the campaign one firm alone sold 300 gallons more milk a day than they did before   That campaign is now going on in other cities of the state, and this kind of work carried on thru the boys and girls, going back in a practical direction to the home and utilized in this fashion is going to be some of the guidance that we need for home-making and for the upbuilding of the boys and girls that are in our schools

If Indiana is going forward it is going because we reach boys and girls, and because we train them in the right way   We have a lot of fathers and mothers who simply think of men and women who go out from our institutions as persons who have not had the experience they have had, who have not spent the years in agriculture that they have spent, and therefore they feel they are not in position to give them much instruction But when we reach boys and girls with such demonstrations as the raising of pigs, cattle, colts, and chickens and when they can carry this knowledge home and demonstrate for themselves that it is a profitable, worth-while thing to do, then we know that better methods are coming on the farms, and in the homes, and there is a changed attitude and a changed life   And then the bigger thing is that it is interesting the parents and showing the worth-whileness of education, and showing them that the teachers and the schools can do these things for boys and girls if they will only support them

We are in position, thru the Industrial Commission, to give assistance to rural communities and give assistance to cities in the securing of funds to hire teachers who will give their attention and their time to this vocational guidance work   Thru the national department and the state institution, we are giving help in boys' and girls' clubs   Thru the State Department of Public Instruction and thru the Federal Board of Vocational Education, we are establishing and conducting now these vocational departments   With this large force working and cooperating and reaching boys and girls, going into the homes, getting hold of the parents and getting them to do the big things, I am sure that vocational work is going to become a reality   And when we have vocational work in all these schools teaching the children to plow, teaching them to feed stock, teaching them how to cook and sew, showing them how to work in the shop, showing them how to do worth-while things, then we are going to have come true in Indiana those lines of President Lawrence

"One goes to school not so much to gain knowledge as to gain power, not so much to learn to know, as to learn to do things"

WHY CHILDREN REACH THE JUVENILE COURT

FRANK J. LAHR, Judge of the Juvenile Court Indianapolis

The subject that has been assigned to me I am a little bit suspicious, was selected by somebody maybe in a spirit of irony. "Why Children reach the Juvenile Court" is the question that I have asked in the last few years thousands of times. I have asked it of people who come into the court and I have asked it of people outside of the court in meetings where I have talked. It is a wonderfully interesting question to think about. In the first place, it is so entirely different from what people think it is.

If I had more time here this afternoon, I should like to ask you, or let you and me together study the question "Why Children reach the Juvenile Court", but the time is short.

First I will say that the people who come before me in the Juvenile Court, and of whom I ask the question, "Why does your boy or your girl reach the Juvenile Court?" invariably answer, "We don't know." That is always the answer. It comes with such uniformity and such positiveness that we are sometimes startled at the fact that people should know so little about why a child reaches the Juvenile Court. And generally, before I have time to ask any more questions, the parents of the child will say to me, "We have done everything we can do." We want you, Judge to know that. They don't say this last, but that is the attitude,—we want you, the judge, to know that we have done everything we can do. That is a strange answer to give, because it is so discouraging. If they have done everything they can do, then there seems to be absolutely no hope further.

In talking before a number of audiences at different places, I have asked the audience the same question. I thought surely the people who are not parents of children who come before the Juvenile Court could tell me, and I would like to ask you the question this afternoon.

In one audience which was a representative audience, a very fine audience of mothers—W C T U women -just as intelligent an audience as any I ever stood before I asked them to study, think it over, and tell me why a boy reaches the Juvenile Court. They were lost. The question was too little understood.

Then I said, "Tell me why a boy steals. Let us limit it to one class of offenses. Why does a boy steal?" I gave them time to study. After sufficient time was given, the answers came. Hands were up. The first five answers that came to me were that stealing comes from the devil. That was not very encouraging to me because that immediately meant that I would have to make my fight with that personality. The next two answers that came were that it comes to the child by heredity. That, too, is a discouraging answer to me, because if it comes by heredity that is something that is already fixed, and neither the Juvenile Court nor anybody else can do anything with it. I have always been suspicious that the two mothers who said that it came by heredity were widows.

Then, as I went down the line for other answers, some would blame the neighboring boy and some would blame one thing and some would blame something else. But in no place, it seemed to me, did the blame fall where it could be of help to me, or where it should be placed.

Now, I want to work on that problem a little bit here this afternoon. I want to take up the question of stealing so as to make it concrete. Why does a boy steal? The answer that it comes from the devil or by heredity, I think, can be disposed of easily. You needn't worry long with those answers. It is a different question from that.

If you want to know why a boy steals, you will have to study the question not from your point of view, but from the point of view of a child. If you want to know why you steal, or rather why you do not steal, if you do not steal, you will have to go back to your own childhood days to study the question. In fact even if you go back to your childhood and work it out at that point, it will not be as clear to you as it should be.

Now, while we are with the child, let us determine, if we can, why it steals. Let us take a child, for instance, two years of age. Does that child then steal or does it not steal? Let us take a child one year of age. Does a child at one year of age steal or does it not steal? I know we are all tender with children, and this word "steal" is odious. Let us change the word. Does the child at one year of age take things or does it not take things? What do you say? How many say it takes things? How many say it does not take things? (Audience unanimous that it does take things.) What does it take? Everything it can lay its hands on. The little child begins stealing as soon as it is big enough to use its hands and feet, and then it takes everything that it can possibly lug away.

What is true of stealing is true of many other things that will suggest themselves to you, but I want you now to see how it is a perfectly natural thing in the child to want things and to take them if it can.

I have in my home a child about a year old. (Its mother once said that I shouldn't say the things I am saying about our children, but my wife is now agreed with me that this one nearly a year old takes everything it can get its hands on and is perfectly willing that I should tell it.) I have one two and a half nearly three years of age now. This little one three years of age doesn't take so many things. It takes a few things. It is constantly getting in trouble with its mother and the rest of the family by reason of its taking things it should not take, but it doesn't take so many things.

I have one seven years of age. This little one seven years of age we would say is a pretty good child. She lets most things alone, not everything but most things. I have a boy twelve years of age. This boy is even better than the girl of seven. He lets most things alone, but not all things; he still takes some things he ought to let alone.

Now, what is it in the child that makes him steal, or what is it that has come into him that keeps him from stealing? If you want to know why the child does not steal, you must study this child that is taking things, this child a year old, or some child at the beginning of life, and compare it with the child that is six or seven or eight or ten years of age, and see what the difference is and find out what has caused the difference.

I am going to ask you what has come into the life of the child three years of age or the child seven years of age or eleven years of age, by which they do not steal so much; they do not take things so much as the little one that is one year of age. What is it that causes such a difference of conduct?

"Training," you say, "education," "being taught the rights of others." I hope that you see the wisdom of your answers, because I want to build out on them as a foundation, and if you don't see it, you will become doubtful after a while and refuse to follow me. But you are right about it. He gets honesty thru teaching, and he gets it no other way except thru teaching. The child learns thru teaching to keep his hands off of people's property, and he gets it no other way.

If it comes to the child thru teaching, instead of from the devil or by heredity, then I am very much encouraged, because if in the Juvenile Court I find a boy who is taking things I know what that boy needs. More teaching. Does he need to be sent off to prison? No. Does he need a whipping? No. I am not going to settle the question now as to whether or not those things might help, but just whether or not they will do the work. They will not make him honest, he needs teaching.

Now, what is true of stealing is also true of the many other things that we accuse children of, and the children are brought before the Juvenile Court in Marion county or before the Juvenile Court in each home, because the juvenile court in each home is not very different from the Juvenile Court in Marion county,—it is the same kind of a court, and there should be in every home a juvenile court in which these cases are tried, and that will save them from going to the state court.

He gets honesty thru teaching. He gets it no other way. If he has not got it, he has not had a good teacher. I wish I had time to give more demonstrations of that proposition.

Who is the one who should do this teaching? You all say the parents. That is right. The parents should be the teacher first of all. Then the teaching of the parents, of course, is reinforced by the teacher at the school. One stands right back of the other. And then it is again reinforced by the Sunday School teacher and by the minister at the church, and then it is again reinforced by the state of Indiana thru its police officers. In that respect, the police officer could be, if he would, a great ethical instructor, occupying a position right alongside the school teacher and the preacher and the mother and the father, because the state thru the police officer is also reinforcing the work that the mother and father have done in the home, or should have done.

Now, then if you ask me why children come to the Juvenile Court, with this foundation laid, the answer is not so hard, is it? You will see it more clearly if you will leave the Juvenile Court and the children who come to the Juvenile Court and go into the families outside of the Juvenile Court and study the question as to why children do not come to the Juvenile Court.

The children in Marion county who do not come to the Juvenile Court are these children who have good fathers and mothers for teachers, and I want to tell you it is true, it is scientifically true. You can observe thousands of cases and make your deductions, the children who come to the Juvenile Court for stealing, or for any of the offenses of which they are accused, come there because their parents have not properly taught them, their mothers and fathers are not good teachers.

One thing I want to call your attention to while you are studying these questions, and that is there is a great big difference between being a teacher and being a father or a mother. It is not the same function at all. There are men and women who are parents, who are fathers and mothers, but they are very poor teachers There are many men and women in Indianapolis who live in the better parts of the city out on North Meridian street, up around Fall Creek and this aristocratic part that you hear about when you come here —there are parents there who are good business people, they are good church people they are good individuals, good citizens, we may say considered in themselves , but when it comes to their ability to teach their children they are not teachers So don't allow yourselves to be fooled that it is only because a child is in a bad family that he becomes a thief or becomes a delinquent child

I want to reinforce this idea I wish I had time, but I haven't, so I will just have to run over it right rapidly Many years ago you who have studied your history carefully will know, when the world was young and there was no civilization here, mankind was in the same condition as the little baby who is born in my house It knows nothing, and they knew nothing From that time on mankind had to begin to work out its problems of civilization, among them the question of property rights The question of property rights was not handed to man by God · man worked it out I want you to observe the fact, by comparison at least that God made wheat and corn and ragweeds and snakes and frogs, but God did not make wheat fields, God did not make fences, God did not make the fruit to grow in fields That is the product of man That is the work of civilization In the same way mankind had to work out property rights It is a convention It is something that the natural man knows nothing about It is something that the natural child knows nothing about It grew out of time I wish I had time to demonstrate this, but I haven't

Now, when the little baby is born into our civilization, in 1919, remember he is born in the condition of primitive man and he must learn all that civilization has and as the generations came and went, one generation handed down to the next generation a little of its civilization It became cumulative A residuum was left for each generation, and it accumulated until now in the year 1919 we have a large accumulation of civilization But remember it didn't come by nature It will have to be handed to each generation from parent to child So I want you to see just exactly as we have seen that honesty is taught from parent to child The whole of civilization is transferred from parent to child, generation by generation, not only on the question of property, not only on the question of honesty, not only on the question of labor and work but on every question which is involved in civilization

In the Juvenile Court, I am a student of general history Every case that comes in there I can classify as to its location in civilization Some belong to a time long before Christ some belong to the primitive times, some come after Christ I can locate them somewhere Then we have to take them at the place we find them and begin the processes of civilization, and the process of civilization is what kind of a process? Teaching

God didn't make civilization We pass it from one man to the other thru teaching God didn't make civilization, but He did make something else of greater importance, and He has a bigger and a more forceful hand in it than we sometimes think.

When a little pig is born the second day after that pig is born, or even the first day sometimes, at least by the second day the little pig can run about and take care of itself. It is almost of age. When a little bird is born, it will stay in the nest three or four weeks, and then it is of age. It has three weeks of infancy. In the case of a pup, why, the second day he is a graduate. He knows it all. He gets stronger and bigger, but there is nothing that he learns any more after the second day.

Look at a child. A little child two days old is not of age. A little child two months old is not of age. A little child two years old is not of age, I mean, does not act for itself. Why, we won't even let a child leave to go to the school teacher before it is six years old and some think it should not go as soon as that. Physiology and anatomy says that a child isn't mature until it is twenty-two or twenty-four years of age. The lawyers weren't close students of anatomy and so they fixed the age at twenty-one, and so the statute says that at twenty-one years of age a child may cut the apron strings, leave the home. The fact that a child was created with an infancy that runs so long was so created by God's own hands—makes you see the purpose of it? Can you see why it was done? When a little pig is born, the mother pig doesn't concern itself about handing its civilization over from the mother pig to the little pig. When the little puppy is born, there is no such discussion as handing civilization over from the mother dog to the little puppy. But in the human race, isn't it interesting that for twenty-one or twenty-two years that child is to stay with the father and mother, is intended to stay right there, and for what purpose? So that the father and mother may teach the child.

Now, in these last few minutes I have, I want to urge you who are parents here to see that the school teachers who are meeting in this grand association over here in the city of Indianapolis do not have a monopoly of teaching. They do not, they are not even the big teachers—they are mighty big, and I respect them, and no one can respect them more than I do, but I want you to know right now that the school teachers are not the big teachers. So far as the teaching process is concerned, the school teacher is simply a reinforcement of what the parents are teaching. The big teachers of the child are the parents.

I want you to be sure to get the idea that I don't undervalue anything that the school does or the church or the business world or the state or all these other institutions that are pouring their great instruction into the life of the child, but I want you to see that this mother comes way up in the life of the child as the teacher. I am a teacher, too. We teachers see it, but mothers do not see it. If we could only get the fathers and mothers to see that they are the great teachers, the great civilizers, that they are the ones who are to do the great foundation work of handing civilization over from themselves to the children, and the school teacher teaches arithmetic and grammar and geography and history, which is an extra, and the church teaches religion which is an extra, but the great work is done by the parents—if we could get parents to see that, then a great deal of trouble about what boys and girls are doing would all pass away. You wouldn't need a Juvenile Court at all if parents could see that thing.

I want to say to my mind there is no greater institution than a parent-teacher association. I think parents and teachers should both wake up, and especially parents should wake up as to the great fact of the teaching power which they have in their homes, and that they and the teacher are both teachers working together for the civilization, for the growth and civilization of the child

THE RURAL SCHOOLS

W. W. BLACK, Professor of Elementary Education in Indiana University (in absence of President WILLIAM LOWE BRYAN)

I have time only to call the attention of this body to a problem that we must attack with all our might   That is the problem of the rural school

Public school education has never been tried as it is being tried today   We are making an attempt in America to rise into the next step in democracy, and as a mass we do not know how to make this step   Our feeling for democracy has run so far ahead of our knowledge of democracy that we are in a sort of blind rush without having clearly in mind the goal, or its direction, or its distance   There is no cut-and-dried method in the development of democracy, so we find ourselves going the costly trial-and-error way   As it seems to me we shall have to hold things in check now and then by the strong arm of state and federal government, until our public education reaches such a degree of efficiency as will enable us to move more intelligently in our rise in democracy. We must consider more seriously than we have in the past that the public schools are the safeguard of democracy; that the schools are the basis for developing a democratic leadership and an intelligent following that will make it possible for us to live together in a democratic way

Our cities have developed a plan of school organization that should in the future make the city schools highly efficient   Our rural schools have no such advantage in organization   They have not only, for lack of proper organization, failed to keep up with the advance made in the city schools, but on the whole they have lost ground   Especially is this true of the one-teacher schools   A quarter of a century ago a very large percentage of teachers in our one-teacher schools were mature men and women of experience   As a rule they remained for a number of years in the same school, and very many of them identified themselves with the life and interests of the community   Now the average length of time the teacher remains in the same one-teacher school is hardly two years   It is our beginning teachers who are teaching in the one-room schools   They are without personal supervision   They are working fewer months a year, and for less salary than are teachers in other schools   They generally lack in social opportunities   Their interests are elsewhere   In very many instances they are unable to secure room and board in the district   Many live in the district only from Monday morning until Friday at four   Practically all are waiting for opportunity to secure better positions elsewhere   Those who succeed well are generally taken by the towns and cities   The consolidated schools are more efficient than are the one-teacher schools but are in general less efficient than the city schools

The country folk know that these things are true   For these and other causes, most of which can be remedied only thru the improved rural school, country folk are leaving the rural community in large numbers   In the period between 1900 and 1910, 74 of the 92 counties of the state lost in rural population. And 56 counties lost in their total population. Of these 56 counties, 53 had no city of 10,000 population and 38 had no city of 5,000. Farmers are moving to the cities for the educational and social advantages they can give their families. Hundreds of families in Indiana who still live on the farm are sending their children to schools in the larger towns and to the cities. We are educating them under a city environment, where they form city habits, city tastes, city interests. When a country child is educated under these conditions, the chances are very much against his returning to permanent rural life.

The problem of the rural school is our most pressing educational problem. It should concern the city dweller as much as those who live in the country district. I am glad to have had opportunity to present conditions to this body of representatives, however briefly, because it is just such bodies as yours that must take an active interest in securing an efficient reorganization of the rural schools.

Appendix

SURVEY OF HIGH SCHOOL LIFE AND CONDITIONS IN FORT WAYNE, IND

The Fort Wayne High School Parent-Teacher Club is organized for service.

Intelligent, effective service must be based on a thoro knowledge of the selected field of action.

The responsibility for directing the policy, the influence, and the action of this organization lies largely with the executive committee.

It is therefore imperative that all members of the executive committee at once become thoroly conversant with high school life and conditions.

I Teachers

Number of men	Number married
Number of women	Number single
Length of service in Fort Wayne	
Salaries	

II Pupils

Total number	Number girls		Number boys
Freshmen	Boys	Girls	
Sophomore	Boys	Girls	
Junior	Boys	Girls	
Senior	Boys	Girls	

III High School Building

Number and size of rooms
Approximate number of children in classes
Number of recitations a day
Conditions of walls and decorations
Toilets
Cloakrooms
Light
Ventilation
Heat
Get plan for new addition

IV Lunchroom

A Food—
    1 Quality
    2 Variety
    3 Price
    4 Service

B Number of pupils served
C Conduct of pupils
D Facilities for conducting a lunch-room

V. *School Organizations*

A. Within school or recognized by school authorities—
  1. Name
  2. Purpose
  3. Boys or girls or both
  4. Place of meeting
  5. Meet how often
  6. Qualifications for membership
B. Organizations of high school pupils not recognized by school authorities—
  1. Name
  2. Purposes

VI. *Athletics and Physical Training*

A. Boys' teams   Girls' teams
B. Physical training
C. Facilities for athletics and physical training

VII. *Auditorium*

How often used for school activities
Classification of these activities
How often used for public purposes

VIII. *Miscellaneous*

High school music
High school dress
Conduct of pupils in high school
Suggestions from teachers in regard to matters of discipline in which
  parental influence would be beneficial
Note: Committees reported on each of these subjects.

SUGGESTED CONSTITUTION AND BY-LAWS FOR LOCAL PARENT-TEACHER ASSOCIATIONS

(adapted from constitution suggested by the Indiana Parent-Teacher Association and the constitution and by-laws of the Rose Hill High School Parent-Teacher Association of Jeffersonville, Ind.)

ARTICLE I

Name

The name of this organization shall be the Parent-Teacher Association of the ———— school, and it shall be affiliated with the state and national organization.

ARTICLE II

Purpose

The purpose of this association shall be to bring the home and school together in the interest of the child, that parents and teachers may coöperate more intelligently in the education of the child.

ARTICLE III

Membership

The membership of this association shall be composed of the patrons and teachers of this school district and anyone interested in the purposes for which the association stands

ARTICLE IV

Officers

The officers of this association shall be a president, vice-president, secretary, and treasurer.

ARTICLE V

Amendments

This constitution may be amended at any regular meeting of the association by a two-thirds vote of the members present, provided notice has been given at a previous meeting

BY-LAWS

ARTICLE I

Rules

Roberts' *Revised Rules of Order* shall govern the proceedings of this association

ARTICLE II

Elections

Officers shall be elected at the last meeting in the spring to hold office one year   Officers shall be nominated from the floor and elected by ballot

ARTICLE III

Duties of Officers

It shall be the duty of the president to preside at all meetings of this association and have general oversight of the affairs of the association The president shall be ex officio member of all committees

The vice-president shall preside in the absence of the president and in a general way assist the president in the affairs of the association

The secretary shall keep an accurate record of all meetings of the association, conduct its correspondence, and perform such other duties as usually devolve upon such an office.

The treasurer shall receive and have charge of all money, shall pay out same on order signed by the secretary and president, keep an account of all receipts and disbursements, and make a written report to each annual meeting   The treasurer shall remit promptly the state and national dues

ARTICLE IV

Committees

(Such standing committees may be provided for here as desired and their method of appointment indicated)

ARTICLE V

Duties of Committees

(The duties of committees should be clearly stated here.)

ARTICLE VI

Dues

(The association must decide whether or not to have dues and if so what amount. This matter should be determined by a membership vote.)

ARTICLE VII

Meetings

This association shall meet on the —————— of each month at the school building.

ARTICLE VIII

Order of Business

Roll call, minutes, program reports, unfinished business, new business.

ARTICLE IX

Amendments

These by-laws may be amended at any regular meeting of the association, provided a notice has been given at a previous meeting.

SUGGESTED CONSTITUTION FOR PARENT-TEACHER COUNCILS IN COUNTIES AND CITIES

(adapted from constitution suggested by the Indiana Parent-Teacher Association and by the National Congress of Mothers and Parent-Teacher Associations)

ARTICLE I

Name

The name of this organization shall be the (name of county or city) Council of Parent-Teacher Associations.

ARTICLE II

Object

The object of this council shall be to carry on the work of the state and national parent-teacher associations, and to bring into closer relationship the local parent-teacher associations, to coordinate their efforts, and to increase their efficiency.

ARTICLE III

Membership

The membership of this council shall be composed of members of the individual parent-teacher associations forming the council.

ARTICLE IV

Officers

There shall be a president, vice-president, secretary, and treasurer who must be members of individual associations forming the council, and who shall perform the usual duties of such officers.

ARTICLE V

Meetings

The council shall hold three meetings a year at times and places to be determined by its officers

ARTICLE VI

Dues

No dues shall be paid by the members of the council, but voluntary offerings may be received if desired

ARTICLE VII

Amendments

This constitution may be amended at any regular meeting of the council by a two-thirds vote of the members present, provided that each local parent-teacher association in membership has been notified of such proposed amendment at least thirty days prior to the meeting at which the amendment is presented

CONSTITUTION AND BY-LAWS OF THE INDIANA PARENT-TEACHER ASSOCIATION

ARTICLE I

Name

The name of this organization shall be the Indiana Parent-Teacher Association, a branch of the National Congress of Mothers and Parent-Teacher Associations

ARTICLE II

Object

The object of this organization shall be to unify and strengthen each force represented in the individual organizations of which it is composed. It shall act as a bureau of information and shall help all organizations which are working in the interest of better homes, better schools, and the welfare of the children of our state   It shall cooperate with educators and legislators, in securing better laws for the mental, moral, and physical development of the child, and for better schools, better paid teachers, and the widest possible use of all public school buildings to the end that good citizenship may be secured and the youth of our state and nation safeguarded

ARTICLE III

Membership

SECTION 1   The membership of this organization shall be composed of associations auxiliary to the public schools of this state, and such other Child Welfare organizations or sections of associations as shall be approved by the executive board.

SEC 2   Educational organizations not organized as parent-teacher associations. but desiring to cooperate in the work, may upon the approval of the executive board, affiliate with the state Parent-Teacher Association upon the payment of a sum as provided for in Art. IV, Sec. 4, of By-Laws.

SEC 3.   The State Superintendent of Public Instruction, County Superntendents, and Superintendents of City Schools shall be honorary members of the State Parent-Teacher Association

ARTICLE IV
Officers

SEC 1 The officers of this organization shall be a president, vice-president at large, a vice-president of each district in the state, executive secretary, recording secretary, treasurer, and auditor who with the exception of the executive secretary shall be elected by ballot biennially

SEC 2 Only active members shall be eligible to office

SEC 3 No person shall hold the same office longer than two consecutive terms

SEC 4 No person shall hold more than one state office at the same time

SEC. 5. There may be honorary vice-presidents, elected in recognition of distinguished services given.

ARTICLE V
Districts

SEC. 1 The state shall be divided according to congressional districts.

SEC 2 The state executive board shall appoint the president of each district, who shall be a vice president of the state, until such a time as there are sufficient organized counties in the district to elect their own officers

SEC 3 The state president or her representative shall call the meetings of the district.

SEC 4. The officers of the district shall be president, recording secretary, and treasurer.

SEC 5 The president of each congressional district shall be a vice-president of the state

ARTICLE VI
Counties

SEC. 1. Each district shall be divided into counties to conform in boundary lines to the counties of the state of Indiana unless otherwise determined by the state executive board

SEC 2 Every parent-teacher association member in good standing shall be a member of the county, district, state, and national organizations, and shall be given all privileges and courtesies of the state conventions except the right to vote on matters of administration, which right shall be given to delegates only.

SEC. 3. In any county in which there are three parent-teacher associations affiliated with the state, a county council may be formed. The meeting to form such a council shall be called by the state president or her representative Until there are three affiliated associations in each county, the executive board shall appoint the president of each county.

SEC 4 The officers of the county council shall be president, vice-president, secretary, and treasurer, and they shall be elected annually at the regular meeting of the council.

SEC 5   Each county shall be divided according to township lines. These units shall be presided over by a township chairman

SEC 6   The voting body of the county council shall consist of the president, vice-president, secretary, treasurer, township chairman president, and secretary of each local parent-teacher association, and one delegate for every ten paid members.

ARTICLE VII
Cities

SEC 1   In each city where there are three or more parent-teacher associations affiliated with the state, there may be organized by the county president or her representative, a city council similar in plan to the county council

ARTICLE VIII
Advisory Council

SEC. 1   There shall be an advisory council of not less than ten, nor more than fifteen members elected biennially by the state executive board, and they shall meet at the call of the president

ARTICLE IX
Boards

SEC 1   There shall be an executive board composed of the officers of the Indiana Parent-Teacher Association, the president of each county, presidents of districts president of the board of department chairmen, and six members elected biennially

SEC 2   There shall be a board of department chairmen, composed of the chairmen of state departments, and they shall elect officers biennially at the state convention

ARTICLE X
Annual Meeting

SEC 1   There shall be an annual meeting of this organization held at the same time and place as the Indiana State Teachers' Association

SEC 2   Twenty-five voting delegates shall constitute a quorum in any state convention

SEC 3   The executive secretary of the Indiana Parent-Teacher Association shall thirty days prior to each state convention, notify each member of the executive board each county president, each department chairman, and the president of each local parent-teacher association, of the exact time and place of the said meeting

ARTICLE XI
Amendments

This constitution may be amended or revised at any annual convention without previous notice, by a two-thirds vote of the registered delegates.

ARTICLE XII
Authority

Roberts *Rules of Order* shall govern the proceedings of this organization.

BY-LAWS

ARTICLE I

SEC 1 There shall be departments in the Indiana Parent-Teacher Association to correspond to those in the national Each state chairman shall be a member of the corresponding committee in the national

ARTICLE II

SEC 1 The executive board shall elect such honorary vice-presidents as may in its judgment serve the best interest of the state

SEC. 2 The executive board shall annually appoint the chairman of each department

SEC 3 The executive board shall constitute the program committee for the annual convention with power to add to its membership

SEC 4 The executive board shall have power to make rules for the transaction of the business of the board and to amend the same from time to time as may prove necessary

SEC 5 The president of the state Parent-Teacher Association shall have the power to appoint such special committees as shall be necessary for the execution of the state work and the safe conduct of the state meeting

SEC 6 The president shall be a member ex officio of all committees

ARTICLE III

SEC 1 The executive board shall meet once before and once after the state convention and at the call of the president, providing notice has been given each member at least two weeks previous to said meeting

SEC 3 Members of the executive board who are obliged to be absent from the meetings shall report in writing to the secretary at least two days before said meeting

SEC 4 Any member of the executive board absenting herself from three consecutive meetings may be considered as having forfeited her membership on the board, unless she has presented to the secretary a valid excuse in writing, as herein provided for

ARTICLE IV

SEC 1 Parent-teacher associations, mothers' clubs, and child welfare circles may affiliate with the state in the following manner

SEC 2 An organization of less than 50 members may affiliate upon the payment of 10 cents per member per year

SEC 3 An organization of 50 members or more may affiliate with the state upon the payment of a flat club rate at $5 per year.

SEC 4 All other organizations shall, upon the approval of the state board pay the treasurer $3 annually, for state dues

SEC 5 Dues shall be payable annually upon the date of admission to the state

SEC 6 The state treasurer shall remit to the national treasurer five cents for every paid membership, and one-half of every affiliated membership

SEC. 7 Each new parent-teacher association, mothers' club, and child welfare circle of fifty members joining the state shall, upon receipt of the names and addresses of officers and members, receive one copy of the *Welfare Magazine* for one year

SEC. 8   Each organization in membership in the state shall receive the state and national Year-Books, and such other literature helps as are available

ARTICLE V

SEC 1   Officers shall be elected biennially at an annual meeting on the last morning of the convention

SEC. 2   Nominations shall be from the floor

SEC 3   Elections shall be by ballot; a majority of all votes cast shall be required to elect

ARTICLE VI

SEC 1   The membership of this organization shall consist of active, associate, sustaining, benefactors, and life members

SEC 2   Parent-teacher associations, mothers' clubs, and child welfare circles, upon the payment of dues as herein stated, shall become active members.

SEC 3   Individuals may become associate members of the state, upon the payment of $1 annually

SEC 4   Individuals may become sustaining members of the state upon the payment of $5 annually

SEC 5   Individuals may become life members of the state upon the payment of $25

SEC 6   The payment of $50 constitutes the payee a benefactor of the Indiana State Parent-Teacher Association

ARTICLE VII

SEC 1   The Indiana Parent-Teacher Association shall be entitled to send to the national convention its president, recording secretary, executive secretary, treasurer or their representative and one delegate for every 1,000 members.

SEC 2   Each parent-teacher association, mothers' club or child welfare circle shall be entitled to send to the state convention its president and one delegate for every 10 paid members   This does not prevent every member from attending the state convention and participating in all the privileges except that of voting, which is given to delegates only.

SEC 3   Affiliated organizations are entitled to send to the state convention their president or one delegate

ARTICLE VIII

SEC 1   These By-Laws may be amended at annual meeting, without previous notice, by a two-thirds vote of those present

ARTICLE IX

SEC 1   Roberts' *Rules of Order* shall govern the proceedings of this organization

CHILD WELFARE STUDY TOPICS

The following suggested topics for study of child welfare by parent-teacher associations are arranged in three groups   (1) topics for study of problems of children of school age in the home and school, (2) topics for study of problems of children under school age in the home, and (3) topics for study of problems of children of all ages in the community Under each topic are given references as sources of definite information Those references marked (*) can be supplied by the Extension Division of Indiana University.

Suggested Topics for Study of Problems of Children of School Age in Home and School

I. Play, Physical Education, Recreation
  1 Legal Provisions in Indiana
    a Burns Revised Statutes of 1914, Laws on Parks, Playgrounds, and Physical Education in the Schools
  2. Physical Education
    a Present Law for Physical Education in the Schools, Acts of 1919, Indiana Legislature, Chapter 149, page 682
    *b Physical Education in the Schools, Bulletin No. 36, 1918 Department of Public Instruction, State of Indiana, Statehouse Indianapolis, Ind
  3 Play
    *a Let the Children Play, 1920, Extension Division, Indiana University, Bloomington, Ind
    *b The Recreation Movement Reprinted from The Playground October, 1911, Playground and Recreation Movement of America, 1 Madison Avenue, New York City
    *c National Games Reprinted from The Playground, December 1911, Playground and Recreation Movement of America, 1 Madison Avenue New York City
    *d Athletic Badge Test for Boys, Athletic Badge Test for Girls, Reprinted from The Playground, April, 1913, Playground and Recreation Movement of America, 1 Madison Avenue New York City.
    *e Health, Morality, and the Playground, Reprinted from Charities and Commons, August 3 1907, by the Playground Association of America and Playground Extension Committee of Russell Sage Foundation New York City
    *f A Year's Campaign for a Life rather than a Living for Everyone in America, Playground and Recreation Association of America, 1 Madison Avenue, New York City
    *g Peace Celebrations for a Better Democracy, Indiana University, Extension Division, Bloomington, Ind
    *h. Play and Recreation, Bulletin of the Extension Division, Indiana University Bloomington Ind Vol II, No 1, Vol I, No 2 (two bulletins)
    *i Patriotic Play Week, Suggestions to Local Child Welfare Committees, U S Department of Labor, Children's Bureau, Washington, D C, Children's Year Leaflet No 4, Bureau Publication No 44, 1918.

j Suggested Procession and Pageant for the Patriotic Play Week, prepared by C H Gifford Executive Secretary of the Drama League of America, Washington D C 1918, Children's Bureau U S Department of Labor

II   Child Labor and Education
   1   The Present Child Labor Law in Indiana
      a. Laws Concerning Children, March 1, 1914, Board of State Charities, 93 Statehouse Indianapolis, Ind
   2   The Present Federal Child Labor Law
      a Tax on Employment of Child Labor (T D 2823), Treasury Department, Office of Commissioner of Internal Revenue, Washington D C
      b Laws Relating to the Employment of Women and Children, Issued by the Industrial Board of Indiana, Department of Women and Children, 1919, Mrs A T Cox, Director
   3   Standards Set at the Washington Conference for Children Entering Employment
      a Minimum Standards for Child Welfare, 1919, U S Department of Labor Children's Bureau, Conference Series No 2 Bureau Publication No 62, pp 3, 4, 5.
      b Standards of Child Welfare, Separate No 2, Child Labor, U S Department of Labor, Children's Bureau, Report from Conference Series No 1, Bureau Publication No 60, 1919)
   4   Child Labor Laws of Other States
      a The States and Child Labor, U S Department of Labor, Children's Bureau Washington, D C Children's Year Leaflet No 13, Bureau Publication No 58
   5   The Proposed Child Labor Law for Indiana
      a Child Labor Bill, Extension Division, Indiana University
   6   Present Provisions for the Department of Women and Children in Industry in the Industrial Board of Indiana
      a Acts of 1919, Legislature of Indiana, Chapter 58 Sec 2 pp 191-192
   7   Employment Certificates
      a The Employment Certificate System, U S Department of Labor, Children's Bureau, Children's Year Leaflet No 12, Bureau Publication No 56
   8   The Present School Attendance Law in Indiana
      a The Compulsory School Attendance Law Issued by the State Board of Truancy, Statehouse, Indianapolis, Ind
   9   Child Labor and School Attendance
      a Minimum Standards for Child Welfare, 1919 U S Department of Labor Children's Bureau Conference Series No 2 Bureau Publication No 62 pp 3, 4, 5
      b Every Child in School, U S Department of Labor, Children's Bureau, Children's Year follow-up series No 3, Bureau Publication No 64
      c Back to School Drive Blanks, U.S Department of Labor, Children's Bureau.

*d. Back to School, U S Department of Labor, Children's Bureau Children's Year Leaflet No 7, Bureau Publication No 49, 1918

*e. Suggestions to Local Committees for the Back-to-School Drive, U S Department of Labor, Children's Bureau, Children's Year Leaflet No 8, Bureau Publication No 50, 1918

*f. Stay-in-School—Education Pays, A Message to the Boys and Girls of America Dodger U S Department of Labor, Children's Bureau

*g. Scholarships for Children, U.S Department of Labor, Children's Bureau, Children's Year Leaflet No 9, Bureau Publication No 51 1918

10 Vocational Guidance

*a. Some Explanations Concerning the Junior Section of the Indiana Free Employment Service, Suggested Phases of Vocational Guidance for Minors Bulletin No 1, Employment Commission of Indiana, Statehouse, Indianapolis, Ind

*b. Advising Children in their Choice of Occupation and Supervising the Working Child U S Department of Labor, Children's Bureau, Children's Year Leaflet No 10, Bureau Publication No 53

III The Public School System

1 School Laws of the State of Indiana

a Laws of Indiana Relating to the Public School System, 1917 by Benjamin J Burris Office of State Superintendent of Public Instruction, Statehouse Indianapolis

b School Laws enacted by the General Assembly 1919 A Supplement to the School Laws of Indiana 1917, Edition by Benjamin I Burris Office of State Superintendent of Public Instruction Statehouse, Indianapolis, Ind

c Indiana Vocational Education Law Approved February 22, 1913 Amended March 14 1919, State Board for Vocational Education, Statehouse Indianapolis, Ind

2 Course of Study in the Public Schools of Indiana

a State Manual and Uniform Course of Study for the Public Schools of Indiana, Department of Public Instruction, Statehouse Indianapolis Ind

3 Salaries of Teachers

a Pamphlets and leaflets supplied by the State Board of Education, Statehouse, Indianapolis Ind

4 Visiting Teachers

*a The Visiting Teacher, U S Department of Labor Children's Bureau, Children's Year Leaflet No 11 Bureau Publication No 55 1919

IV Health of Children

1 School Feeding

*a Feeding Children at School, Bulletin of Indiana University Extension Division, Vol IV No 8 Bloomington Ind

2 Malnutrition

*a What is Malnutrition, Lydia Roberts, U S Department of Labor, Children s Bureau

3 Health Habits

*a Record of Health Chores, Modern Health Crusades, by National Tuberculosis Association, 381 Fourth Avenue New York City

*b Common Sense in Health, A Health Campaign American Red Cross, Junior Red Cross Washington, D C , A Teachers' Manual Supplement No 3, 1919

4 Sanitation of Buildings and Health Supervision of Children.

a Manual of Instructions for School Authorities and School Physicians, State Board of Health, Statehouse, Indianapolis, Ind , 1911

b The Indiana Medical Inspection of Schools Law, Burns Revised Statutes, 1914

V The School a Social Center

1 Community Instruction

*a Community Institutes , Notes on the Purposes and Method of the Institutes held in 1915-1916, Bulletin of the Extension Division, Indiana University, Bloomington, Ind , Vol II, No 5, January, 1917

2 School Service

*a School and Community Service Experiments in Democratic Organization by Robert E Cavanaugh and Walton S Bittner, Bulletin of the Extension Division, Indiana University, Bloomington, Ind , Vol. IV, No. 6, February, 1919

*b Town and City Beautification , Notes and List of Lantern Slides Bulletin of the Extension Division, Indiana University, Bloomington, Ind Vol IV, No 5 January, 1919

*c The Community Center, Bulletin of the Extension Division, Indiana University, Bloomington, Ind , Vol. V, No 8, April, 1920

3 School Library.

*a. Reference Aids for Schools, Library Movement in the Schools, Bulletin of the Extension Division, Indiana University, Vol I, No 9 May, 1916

4. High School Discussion

*a State High School Discussion League Announcements, Indiana University Bulletin, Vol. XII, No 13, 1915, Extension Division

*b. Compulsory Military Service for the United States, High School Discussion League Announcements, 1916-17, Bulletin of the Extension Division, Indiana University, Vol II, No. 2, October, 1916

*c The Railroad Problem by Adela K Bittner, High School Discussion League Announcements, 1919-20, Bulletin of the Extension Division, Indiana University, Vol V, No 2, October, 1919

VI Thrift.
    1 Teaching Thrift.
        a Outline of Lessons to Teach Thrift in Normal and Training Schools for Teachers, U S Treasury Department, Washington, D C, August, 1919.
        b Outline Suggested for Teaching Thrift in Elementary Schools, Savings Division, U S. Treasury Department, August, 1919
        c Fifteen Lessons in Thrift, Savings Division, U S Treasury Department, August, 1919
        d Ten Lessons in Thrift Savings Division, U.S Treasury Department, Washington, D C, May, 1919

VII. Social Hygiene
    1 Sex Education
        a The Problem of Sex Education in Schools, Indiana State Board of Health Statehouse, Indianapolis, Ind
        b God's Children, by Emma Lieber, Indiana State Board of Health
        c From Girlhood to Womanhood, by Emma Lieber, Indiana State Board of Health
        (Other publications may be had from the State Board of Health)

VIII Open Air Schools
    1. Fresh Air Movement
        a The Open Air School Movement in Indiana, Indiana State Board of Health, and Indiana Tuberculosis Association, K of P. Building, Indianapolis, Ind, October, 1918
        b Other publications by the State Board of Health and the Indiana Tuberculosis Association.

Suggested Topics for Study of Problems of Children under School Age in the Home

I. Protection of Mothers
    1 Prenatal Care.
        *a Prenatal Care—1915, U S Department of Labor, Children's Bureau Washington, D C, Care of Children series No. 1, Bureau Publication No 4

II Protection and Care of Young Children
    1 Care of Infants.
        *a Infant Care—1914, U S Department of Labor, Children's Bureau, Care of Children series No 2, Bureau Publication No 8
        *b To the Mothers of Indiana Indiana State Board of Health. Department of Infant and Child Hygiene, Statehouse Indianapolis, Ind
    2 Care of Children of Pre-school Age.
        *a Child Care—1918, U.S Department of Labor, Children's Bureau, Washington, D C, Care of Children series No. 3, Bureau Publication No 30

3 The Use of Milk
*a Dodger No 7—Milk, U S Department of Labor, Children's Bureau
*b Milk—The Indispensable Food for Children U S Department of Labor, Children's Bureau Care of Children series No 4, Bureau Publication No 35
*c The Foster Mother of the World and Her Relation to Human Nutrition, by James J Harvey General Secretary Indiana Manufacturers of Dairy Products, Indianapolis, Ind

Suggested Topics for Study of Problems of Children of All Ages in the Community

I The Public Protection of the Health of Mothers and Children
1 The Proposed Maternity and Infancy Protection Law
*a The Shepperd-Towner Bill for Public Protection of Maternity and Infancy, Senate Bill No 3259, House Bill No 10925
*b Digest of the Shepperd-Towner Bill, U S. Department of Labor, Children's Bureau, Washington D C, M 637, February, 1920 (1022)
2 Minimum Standards for the Public Protection of the Health of Mothers and Children
*a Minimum Standards for Child Welfare, U S Department of Labor, Children's Bureau, Conference series No 2, Bureau Publication No 62, pp 6-9
b Standards of Child Welfare, Separate No 3, The Health of Mothers and Children U S Department of Labor, Children's Bureau, Reprint from Conference Series No 1, Bureau Publication No 60
3 Maternal and Infant Mortality
*a Save the Youngest, U S Department of Labor, Children's Bureau, Children's Year follow-up Series No 2, Bureau Publication No 61
4 Relation of Low Income to a High Infant Mortality Rate
*a. Income and Infant Mortality, by Julia C. Lathrop, Reprinted from American Journal of Public Health, April, 1919, pp 270-274.
5 Birth Registration
*a Birth Registration Test U S Department of Labor, Children's Bureau, 1916
6 Rural Work
*a. Progress in Rural Work for Infant and Maternal Welfare, U S Department of Labor Children's Bureau
7 Public Health Nurses
*a The Public Health Nurse, How She Helps to Keep the Babies Well, by C E A Winslow, D P H, U S Department of Labor, Children's Bureau, Children's Year Leaflet No 6, Bureau Publication No 47, 1918

8   Baby Saving Campaigns
   *a   Save 100,000 Babies—Get a Square Deal for Children, U S
        Department of Labor, Children's Bureau, Children's Year
        Leaflet No. 1, Bureau Publication No 36, 1918
   *b   April-May Weighing and Measuring Test, Part I, Suggestions
        to Local Communities, U S Department of Labor, Children's
        Bureau, Children's Year Leaflet No 2, Part I, Bureau Publi-
        cation No 38
   *c   April-May Weighing and Measuring Test, Part II, Sugges-
        tions to Examiners, U S Department of Labor, Children's
        Bureau, Children's Year Leaflet No 2 Part II, Bureau
        Publication No 38
   *d   April-May Weighing and Measuring Test, Part III, follow-up
        work U S Department of Labor, Children's Year Leaflet
        No 2, Part III, Bureau Publication No 38, 1918

9   Children's Clinics, Health Centers and Health Conferences
   *a   Children's Health Centers, U S Department of Labor, Chil-
        dren's Bureau, Children's Year Leaflet No 5, Bureau Publi-
        cation No 45, 1918
   *b   How to Conduct a Children's Health Conference, by Frances
        Sage Bradley, M D and Florence Brown Sherbon, M D
        U.S Department of Labor, Children's Bureau Miscellaneous
        Series No 9 Bureau Publication No 23, 1917
   *c   Children's Health Conference Blank for Examination, Exten-
        sion Division Indiana University
   *d   Weighing and Measuring Test, Record Card, 1918, U S
        Department of Labor Children's Bureau

II   Americanization
   1   The Americanization Movement
      *a   The Americanization of America, by Lillian Gay Berry
           Associate Professor of Latin, Indiana University, Americani-
           zation in Indiana, by the Extension Division Staff, Bulletin
           of the Extension Division Indiana University, Vol IV,
           No 11, July, 1919

III   Juvenile Courts
   1   Juvenile Delinquency
      a   Juvenile Delinquency in Rural New York, by Kate Holliday
          Claghorn, U S Department of Labor, Children's Bureau
      b   Courts in the United States Hearing Children's Cases, by
          Evelina Belden U S Department of Labor, Children's
          Bureau, 1918
      c   Children Before the Courts in Connecticut, by Wm B Bailey
          Ph D, U S Department of Labor, Children's Bureau, 1918

IV   Mothers' Pensions
   1   Existing Laws
      a   Law Relating to "Mothers' Pensions" in the United States,
          Canada, Denmark, and New Zealand, by Laura A Thompson,
          U S Department of Labor, Children's Bureau Legal Series
          No 4, Bureau Publication No 63

CPSIA information can be obtained at www.ICGtesting.com
Printed in the USA
LVOW05s0757241113

362604LV00004B/102/P